TRINIDAD HIGH SCHOOL
LIBRARY

D0045894

Neil GAIMAN

ON HIS WORK AND CAREER

Trinidad High School
Library

A Conversation with
Bill Baker

ROSEN
PUBLISHING®

New York

Published in 2008 by The Rosen Publishing Group, Inc.
29 East 21st Street, New York, NY 10010

Copyright © 2008 by William M. S. Baker

The "Neil Gaiman: All He Has to Do Is Dream" interview was conducted
on February 5, 1999, and originally appeared on www.collecting-Comics.
com. "The Last Guardian Angel Visitation" originally appeared in
three installments (October 18, 20, and 23, 2000) on www.WizardWorld.
com, as "The Last Guardian Angel Visitation: 5 Minutes with Neil
Gaiman on the CBLDF & The Last Angel Tour."

Slightly different versions of "Running Down a Dream" and "The Last
Guardian Angel Visitation" previously appeared as "Running Down a
Dream: Neil Gaiman on Stalking the Wild Tale" and "Send Me a Guardian
Angel: Neil Gaiman on Freedom of Expression, Censorship, and the Need
for the CBLDF" in *Sketch* magazine Vol. 3, No. 2, Issue 14, April 2002.

First Edition

All rights reserved. No part of this book may be reproduced in any
form without permission in writing from the publisher, except by a
reviewer.

Library of Congress Cataloging-in-Publication Data

Gaiman, Neil.
Neil Gaiman on his work and career : a conversation with Bill Baker.
    p. cm. — (Talking with graphic novelists)
Includes bibliographical references and index.
ISBN-13: 978-1-4042-1078-3
ISBN-10: 1-4042-1078-4
1. Gaiman, Neil—Interviews. 2. Authors, English—20th century—
Interviews. I. Baker, Bill, 1958– II. Title.
PR6057.A319Z46 2008
823'.54—dc22

          2007009904

Manufactured in the United States of America

Cover photo of Neil Gaiman © AP Image

Table of Contents

Interview

To say that I'm a lucky man is a bit of an understatement.

Not only am I the only journalist who was granted a second interview with Neil Gaiman during his recent book tour to support the release of *Smoke and Mirrors*, I was able to conduct it over a very enjoyable and relaxed dinner. Neil had just woken up and, as he provided a wonderfully vivid description of the dream he'd just had (apparently, there's a group of book-burning censors holding meetings in his attic), we ambled down to a nice little pub in downtown Ann Arbor, just up the street from the Borders Books flagship store where he was to appear that evening. After being seated in a suitably comfortable booth and ordering some hot chocolate and a monstrous plate of nachos, we got down to the business at hand. And, as you're about to discover, the *New York Times* best-selling author of *Good Omens* and *Neverwhere*, as well as the *Sandman* series of graphic novels, proved to be every bit as witty and personable as his increasingly popular and endlessly entertaining tales suggest.

Bill Baker: *You just woke up a few moments ago; how are you feeling?*

Neil Gaiman: I'm still slightly bleary, not quite tracking with reality. But then again, I've never been very good at tracking with reality. But [I'm] more or less here, thanks.

BB: *[laughter] Great. How's the tour going in general? Is this your typical state of mind these days?*

NG: It's been fairly exhausting. It started . . . uhm, when did it start? God, it seems like four or five lifetimes ago. It was only the 8th of January, only about five weeks ago.

BB: *Of course, first you flew out to the West Coast and started there.*

NG: If you were going to describe this tour, you'd get a drunk spider, dip it in ink, and put it on a map of America. It sort of starts in Minneapolis, goes to San Diego, Los Angeles, Denver, Pittsburgh, back to Minneapolis, to Powell's [bookstore] in Portland, up to

Seattle, three days in the [San Francisco] Bay area, followed by a day back home, then Maryland . . . Baltimore, Philadelphia, New York, Dayton [Ohio], Madison, Chicago, here [Ann Arbor], and, after that, I've got to go back to Chicago tomorrow, for the premiere of the play.

BB: *Right.* Signal to Noise *(at the NOWtheatre in Chicago).*

NG: And from there, I go down to Atlanta, and then up to Toronto; we've just added a third signing, in Toronto.

BB: *So, I take it that the book's [*Smoke and Mirrors*] doing well, then.*

NG: Oh, yes. I'm kind of enjoying myself in a very peculiar way, because I'm going around America currently, breaking records in bookstores for signings. I broke Martha Stewart's record at Powell's in Portland. I've broken Ray Bradbury's and my [record] at Stars My Destination [bookstore in Chicago]; every place I've been, I'm somewhere in the top three signings they ever had. And yet, I'm still . . . you know, talk with 90 percent of the people in America and say there's a writer named Neil Gaiman, and they'll ask what name he writes under. Which is . . . I'm starting to *really* enjoy it.

I feel like I'm getting away with something. I feel like I'm operating under the radar. Even just the way the books are selling, it's happening under the radar. Yes, we're popping up on some best-seller lists. We were at number 4 on the *LA Times*, we got onto the *Denver Post*, and so on and so forth. But what seems to be happening is the books are selling in such steady numbers—week in, week out, week in, week out—instead of spiking for the first two weeks and then falling off, which is the way that these things *never* happen. It's like we're doing best-seller numbers, but we're doing it under the radar. *Neverwhere* in paperback hasn't been off the Ingram's top 20 list of fantasies since it was published. Week in, week out, it's number 16, 9, 18, whatever. The books are just quietly shifting.

BB: *It's kind of like Pink Floyd's* Dark Side of the Moon *of books.*

NG: Yeah. And it's not stopped selling. They were telling me at Avon [Books] last week . . . I was asking when they're going to be doing a paperback of *Smoke and Mirrors*; and they said they aren't—at this point. And I said, "Why not?" And they said, "'Cause it's selling so steadily in hard cover." And [yet], when it came out, they were *almost* disappointed, because they expected it to do really, really well, and then it looked like it wasn't. Except that, now—three months later—we're already in our third printing. The copies are going out to bookstores, they're selling, and they keep ordering more.

It's cool, but very, very strange.

BB: *What are the print numbers on those runs?*

NG: I don't know exact printing numbers. I know the first printing on *Smoke and Mirrors* was, I think, 25 or 28 [thousand copies]. First print on *Stardust* was, I think, 55, 60 [thousand], something like that. And first printing on *Neverwhere* in paperback was over a quarter million.

BB: *And you've sold over 300,000 of* Neverwhere *in paperback, right?*

NG: They're in the third printing already.

BB: *Third printing?! Geez . . . !*

NG: But as I say, it's so peculiar, because it all gets to happen under the radar. And there was a very, very short period [where] I was almost irritated by that. And then I thought, "No, I'm really, really not."

I love the sort of strange virtue of anonymity that I have.

BB: *Yeah; you've got enough fame to get you in the door, so to speak, but not so much that they're going to stop you on the street.*

NG: Exactly. Nobody in here is ever going to stop me for an autograph. Except tonight's signing will be a very, very serious Borders [Books] signing, [because this is] a Borders that knows how to do these things.

BB: *It's funny, because I often get stopped by people when I'm wearing your [Sandman character] T-shirts, and they ask, "Is that Death?" You were talking in our last interview about fame, how it's affected you, how every now and then a stock boy will stop you and ask you for your autograph.*

NG: Yeah. It's weird, 'cause I get to be famous to . . . Well, it's like in Hollywood right now. I'm getting to the point where I'm starting to have a certain amount of clout, but it's clout in a very peculiar way. The studio heads haven't a clue who I am, but their assistants worship me like unto a god. [*laughter from BB*] But it's *that* kind of thing. It's those people.

BB: *Which also helps explain how you got in to see the producers in the first place; the assistants, who do most of the work anyway, have said, "Hey, you* need *to, like, check this guy out!"*

NG: Exactly.

BB: *That* is *the best of both worlds, isn't it?*

NG: Right now it is, yes. [*displays a very satisfied smile*] I don't know how balanced it's going to remain.

BB: *Any awards or nominations for* Stardust *yet?*

NG: Not yet. It hasn't been out . . . There are a few I'm hoping for. But none of them [nominations] get announced for another six months.

BB: *How about* Smoke and Mirrors, *or* Neverwhere?

NG: *Neverwhere* got a number of award nominations, and won a few things. It was nominated for a Mythopoeic award; it didn't win, but I'm not going to grumble about that. And Andy [Heidel, who's acting as Neil's signing tour manager at Avon] was telling me about various "Year's Best" lists that we got [included on].
    [*at this point our food arrived—nachos*]

BB: *How's the [Harlan] Ellison short story collaboration coming along?*

NG: Well, I'm looking forward to Harlan sending his bit ASAP. He promised it a few days ago, but he was

actually getting back to work on it. Having said that, it's Harlan's story, for Harlan's book.

BB: Partners in Wonder *[part of the Edgeworks series, reprinting Ellison's entire catalogue, from White Wolf Publishing].*

NG: Exactly. And the thing about having [it be part of] one of Harlan's books, I know sooner or later he's going to have to get down to it, 'cause he'll look at the deadline for *Partners in Wonder* . . .

BB: *It's scheduled for September [1999].*

NG: You see my point. I'll wait; I'll wait for Harlan. It's his story.

BB: *Any thematic or plot details you want to give away? Perhaps the title?*

NG: Current working title is "Cheap Day for Night." And it's about living for free and going to the movies. And, uhm . . . further than that, I'll wait to see what Harlan does next to it to find out what it's about.

BB: *Any other short stories coming out? For instance, I remember a short you read at Mad Con [the Mad Media Con, held in Madison, WI] last year where you*

were writing the story with Harlan, called "Earl's Court: A Love Story" . . .

NG: God, did I read that?! [*Neil seems truly surprised*]

BB: *Yes, you did. It was very well received, in fact; although you* did *seem a bit nervous about it.*

NG: I didn't even know if I'd ever read that in public. Is that scary!

That will be out in an anthology called *999: The Final Anthology*, or something like that, from Avon. It's edited by Al Sarantonio. That'll be out on, of all things, on the 7th of September, 1999. And I said to them, "Why isn't it 9–9–1999?" With a book called *999* it seems like . . . But the shipping date [is set], so it's coming out on 9–7–1999.

BB: *Any other new shorts?*

NG: Just finished one a few days ago, which had the working title of "Harlequin's Valentine," [but it] might not be called "Harlequin's Valentine." And it'll be in the World Horror Convention program booklet. I'm the master of ceremonies at the World Horror Convention.

BB: *This year's, correct?* [*Neil nods*] *And that's in . . .*

NG: March, in Atlanta. Within spitting distance of today.

BB: *Any details about the story you'd like to reveal?*

NG: It's a story from the point of view of an invisible harlequin who has fallen in love with a young lady, and must demonstrate his love. As the story starts, he has cut out his heart and pinned it to her front door.

BB: *So. It's the typical, sentimental . . .*

NG: Typical, sentimental, hearts and flowers . . . It really is. It's a Valentine's Day story. It's one of those that's all about love. And valentines. And harlequins. And the harlequinade.

    Which is a really silly thing to write about, I've discovered, because *absolutely* nobody knows anything about the harlequinade anymore. And, in fact, the *Onion* [the satirical paper], who interviewed me a week or so ago did a gag on it on their front cover. Sort of "Who's your favorite comedia dell'arte character? Harlequin? Scaramouche? Punchinello?" [And the answer is] "I don't know: 100 percent!" I thought, "That's *just* what I need." [*laughter*]

BB: *What's funny is, because of my [theater arts] background, I actually know about the harlequinade, and the rest of it. And even I can't answer that one.*

NG: It's about moving roles through a harlequinade. It's a tale of a harlequin who starts to discover that maybe he's not a harlequin, after all. Maybe he's a Pierrot.

BB: *[after his laughter subsides] How about* Coraline?

NG: *Coraline* needs desperately to be finished. She's currently . . . She's grumpy with me, 'cause I should have finished up by Christmas. And right now, it's just a matter of really wanting to get back to it.

BB: *And hoping she's still speaking with you at that point.*

NG: Yeah. I left her in peril in November ['98].

BB: *Ah, and she's getting a little impatient with you.*

NG: Yup. She's just about to meet a number of small children who've been dead, respectively, about 1,000 years, 600 years, or 300 years, who are locked in a closet with her.

BB: *Any other details about it, other than it's supposed to be a "very, very scary children's story"?*

NG: Yep. No, that's pretty much it, for a quote.
I wanted to write a book for little girls, having some [myself], and for some reason the book I

apparently want to write [for] little girls is a very scary one. I obviously hoped it was going to have ponies in it, perhaps a jolly visit to the seaside, and maybe it could all sort of end at the ballet. I don't think we've got a hope for *any* of those things.

BB: *Any themes that did appear, other than those you'd hoped would appear?*

NG: Apparently, one of the themes is that sometimes boring is more fun than interesting, when you actually get to experience interesting. And that parents can be annoying, but the alternative is much worse. I don't know . . . Obviously, some of these themes are, functionally, rather sort of standard themes of kids' fiction [in general].

But, in my defense, I would say that I never actually sat down and said, "There will be a moral to this story. There will be themes to this story." It's just loving this self-contained little girl, and watching her in dreadful danger.

BB: *Typically, then, it seems you find your themes the same way you find your stories and plots: you just sit down and write?*

NG: I very rarely . . . With *Neverwhere*, I knew I had a theme I wanted to address. You know, one wants to sugarcoat the pill.

Whereas I did an interview yesterday with a journalist from Toronto, or somewhere, who basically was saying he read *Stardust* and could not find a redeeming moral. [That] while he had *enjoyed* it greatly, it obviously did not have a redeeming sort of moral philosophy behind it, and it was not . . . you know, "Why not?"

And all I could do was sort of apologize, really. [*laughter*] It's a fairy story.

Also, at a very real level, with *Stardust*, I was saying the book's [the equivalent of] ice cream. Some things you feel are steak, and some are sushi, and some are ice cream. And the steak, everyone will love. And the sushi, some people won't feel it's to their taste, although you might be very proud of it. And, every now and then, you make ice cream and everyone will like it.

BB: *Something to clear the palate, so to speak.*

NG: Yeah. It's fresh, and silly, and different, and that's what it is. And it's not anything more than that, and if you try to make it something more than that, you'll come up with a bit of a [mess]. *Stardust* is fun.

BB: *How about* American Gods? *Anything new on that?*

NG: I need to start really working in earnest on that when this tour is done. It'll be back to *Coraline,* and then *American Gods.*

BB: *It's still the same basic plot—a road movie with dead gods?*

NG: Yeah. "Road movie with dead gods" is a good way of describing it. Lotsa weird stuff. All those people who came to me 'cause they liked how friendly and ice creamy *Stardust* was, will find themselves placed in an untenable position with *American Gods.*

On the other hand, I hope the *Sandman* fans— who, ever since the *Sandman* was done have been going, "Why doesn't he ever do anything like *that* in his prose?"—will, with any luck, wind up being pleased and thrilled by getting something that makes the nasty bits in *Sandman* look like something not really that nasty when compared to the nasty bits in *American Gods.*

BB: *Of course, you had some nasty bits in* Neverwhere.

NG: Uhm . . . *Neverwhere* has a certain amount of blood, and gore, and what have you, but at the end of the day, it is a *romp.* This one is *not* going to be that much of a romp.

BB: *A little more serious, in a way, then?*

NG: I don't know about serious, but it's not a romp in the same way. *Neverwhere* was a Narnia book. *Neverwhere* was Oz. *American Gods* is gonna be about America; and America is a much nastier place. Or at least it contains nastiness, among the other things it contains.

BB: *Kinda like your steak, then; a nice, rare piece of steak.*

NG: Yeah. Or, to keep the metaphor going completely, it's a lot like a strange sort of nacho dish. [*pointing to the plate before us*] There'll probably be something in *American Gods* to every sort of taste—even if they don't like the olives.

BB: *Let's talk comics for a bit. I wanted to discuss some things that I've never seen you talk about before. Is there a chance of your doing a collection of the graphic short stories you've done in the past, pulling together those oddities like "The Death of Emperor Heliogabolus," "Babycakes," the short piece in the recent issue of* Cherry, *etc.?*

NG: The problem is that so many of these things are owned by different people. And the other problem is the astonishing collapse of the comics market. DC has been talking about collecting my short stuff that

I did for them together . . . but there isn't an awful lot that's not collected.

BB: *Such as the [Poison Ivy and Riddler stories from]* Secret Origins, *and a few other odds and ends . . .*

NG: A few little things, here and there. Then you've got . . . the other stuff you've got a lot of different formats. Some things in color, some in black and white.

I would imagine that, in order to make it happen, I would need to . . . go out, drum up somewhere it could happen. And one wouldn't want to do it with DC, because they'd suddenly want rights to something they don't currently have the rights to do.

BB: *Exactly. The lawyers get involved.*

NG: [And] Kitchen Sink is currently going out of business, and they would have been my other choice. Maybe Dark Horse; I don't know.

BB: *Well, you could always do it through Dream Haven [Books, who published* Angels and Visitations *and Neil's* Babylon 5 *script, "Day of the Dead"], and make it a Comic Fund benefit book.*

NG: A [Comic Book] Legal Defense Fund thing. It's kinda fun handling Legal Defense Fund [projects] there, because it means I can put out things I would worry otherwise were trivial, like the *Babylon 5* script.

BB: *Right, which is a really fun read, by the way. I haven't seen the episode, but the script holds up nicely by itself.*

NG: The *Babylon 5* script is definitely an example, apparently, of an ideal relationship between the Fund and Dream Haven. We split the division of spoils three ways: the Legal Defense Fund gets a third of the profits, I take a third, and Dream Haven takes a third. I don't feel guilty, just because [of] the necessity of pricing something like that—it's a $12 book, for something that's very, very thin. And I don't feel guilty because, uhm . . .

BB: *A greater good is being served?*

NG: Exactly.

BB: *On a somewhat related topic, what about* Sweeney Todd?

NG: I don't know, I've been thinking about that a lot, recently. I'm going to talk with Michael [Zulli] and see if we can figure a way to either get it going again, or . . . 'Cause if we don't, I want to do it myself, either as a novel, or some other project down the line. It's just silly, 'cause I spent so much time researching it, I've now forgotten more about Sweeney Todd than most people will ever know. So, I hope that, at some point, I can go on and finish that.

BB: *Well, if nothing else, maybe you could get Vince [Locke] to ink it.*

NG: He's doing an amazing job on Michael's pencils, currently [on an upcoming *Sandman Presents* story arc]. Have you seen it?

BB: *No, unfortunately not. But the combination of those two is really a nice match [check out the* Witchcraft II *miniseries from Vertigo, for instance].*

Uhm, I don't know if you'll want to talk about this or not; it's about the only question dealing with the Dreaming *characters that I've got for you today. There was a moratorium on other artists using the* Endless *characters for about five years, where you were the only one allowed to write them. Since then, that policy shifted somewhat, so that . . .*

NG: The policy . . . There was never a moratorium; it was always an "ask first" [situation]. You know, you'll find them in little cameos and stuff.

      I just got really annoyed. It was like . . . The first time somebody asked to do a Death cameo, and we said yes, and they didn't do what they promised.

BB: *That was the* Captain Atom *issue?*

NG: Yeah. *Captain Atom.* And not only that, they tried to muck up the whole continuity of the thing.

BB: *Right, she was suddenly an aspect of death.*

NG: She was the *nice* death! And I said, "No. She's not the nice death. That's the whole point of it. She's *Death.*"

      What we discovered [was] people could not be trusted.

BB: *So, they had your permission after telling you what they planned to do, but you didn't get to see what they'd done with it until later.*

NG: What we were told was Captain Atom would die, Death'd show up, say something cute, and he'd go on to the afterlife.

BB: *It's been a while since I've seen the issue, but she was very "California," if I remember correctly.*

NG: Yeah, it was bad.

Since then, there's been the *Destiny* [*Destiny: A Chronicle of Deaths Foretold*] series . . . but then, I didn't create *Destiny*.

BB: *Bernie Wrightson, actually, as far as the visual . . .*

NG: Yeah?

BB: *I just found that out in the recent coverage of Joe Orlando's death.*

NG: I always assumed it was Joe. 'Cause Joe created Lucien, and Joe created Cain and Abel, obviously.

BB: *Apparently, it was Bernie—with Joe's guidance—who first drew him.*

Did you ever see the DC Universe, as it's recently been described, as separate or different from the Vertigo world, or what's become known as Vertigo?

NG: No, I've never really seen it that way. As a matter of fact, when I did *The Wake* [story arc in *The Sandman*], I put Superman, Batman, and the Martian Manhunter and Darkseid and those various characters in "The Wake." It just seemed like they belonged there.

BB: *Also, of course, there were the early appearances of Mister Miracle and Martian Manhunter in* The Sandman *series.*

NG: Not to mention Element Girl, and even Prez.

BB*: You were talking earlier about the Batman stories and other bits you've done in the past; is there an existing character—whether it's at DC, Marvel, or one of the dead [defunct] publishers—is there any character, say, Donald Duck, you'd like to work on?*

NG: [*after laughing at the Duck reference*] Not really. I mean there are . . .

The trouble is, they come with so much baggage. The last time I was really excited by something [like that], I had this idea to do a Batman—no, sorry—Superman story with Matt Wagner. This was in 1990 and 1991.

Plotted the whole thing out. Presented it to DC. And Mike Carlin killed it, because he said he wasn't having two hotshots, you know, an artist and writer, coming in and reaping Superman royalties from the character his guys toiled [over] in the vineyards every day. So it died.

The plot of it was, as I remember it, it took place over four seasons—winter, spring, summer, and fall—and would have had the death of

Superman in it. And it would have been set in a sort of never-neverland; the Fleischer world. Pretty much the Fleischer [animated] Superman.

BB: *Almost the* Superman Adventures *animated look?*

NG: Yeah. Well, actually, long before that look or feel ever happened. Those were the plans we wanted to do, and—looking back—we might have been a bit ahead of our time. But it's also true that Mike Carlin didn't want us doing something cool, and that the regular [Superman] people didn't want us to do it, and I feel for my part . . .

When we were told we couldn't do it, I said, "Fine."

BB: *That's too bad; it almost sounds like a really good Elseworlds tale.*

What do you think about the future of comics? And I'm not just talking about it as an art form here, but also as a profession and as an industry.

NG: As an industry, I think comics destroyed itself in 1992, and nobody noticed.

BB: *Because of any one event, or . . .*

NG: No, by the time I got up in 1993 and made the speech about the Dutch Tulip fiasco, the damage was already done. I mean, they'd already . . .

You've got unscrupulous dealers, selling boxes of twenty-five comics to kids as an investment. You've got unscrupulous publishers, aiming their stuff towards those kids. And it was like some kind of bizarre con, trick, or [pyramid] scheme. It all works fine, until the first person tries to sell their comics.

It's to the point where, great, Marvel sold eight million copies of *X-Men* #1. Five different covers, maximizing their profits. That's fine—until the year and a half later, maybe two years later, [when] the kids [who] have bought their boxes of twenty-five copies of [*X-Men* books] go down to the comic shop and say, "OK. I've got my *X-Men* #1 to sell."

And the guy in the shop says, "We got 600 of 'em out the back."

And [the kid] says, "No, no; you don't understand! I'm willing to sell you my *X-Men* #1! I have 200 of them. What will you give me for them?"

And the guy says, "OK, kid. Let me explain something to you. We have 600 of 'em out the back. We're using them to keep the place warm. We are shredding them and putting them back to keep the draft out." And at that point the bottom, middle, and top fell out of the entire scheme, and never came back. The commercial damage was crippling. The whole thing went into freefall.

You know, I brag about the fact that *Sandman*, by its end, was outselling Batman and Superman. But the way that we were outselling Batman and Superman was 'cause our readership simply stayed level. We'd never sold *Sandman* on the promise of covers and stuff. More to the point, we'd never sold them *Sandman* as things you don't open the bag on.

BB: *Right. They were comics to be read.*

NG: They were to be read. Which meant that, as every-body else started collapsing . . . None of our readers went away. So suddenly we were selling 100,000 before, [and] we were down at, like, number 60 [on Diamond Distributors list of 100 best-selling comics], and suddenly we look round, and we're at number 8 . . . and we're still selling 100,000.

These days, if we were selling 100,000, I'm sure we'd be back at number 1.

BB: *Real close. Really close; it's amazing.*

NG: I don't see it turning around. I don't see it fixing [itself]. I don't see masses of new comic stores open-ing to take the place of the ones that are closing.

There are now a number of American states without a comic store.

Given that . . . *plus* the amount of product now coming out . . . Bizarrely, while the amount of money being spent on everything has gone down—it's probably a third of what it was five years ago—product has tripled. So, whereas before, ten years ago, [with] 800 comic stores internationally, if half of them picked up your comic, you sold 4,000. You were just about breaking even. You could at least cover a black-and-white printing bill.

Now, you could print something and not sell *any*. You could wind up eating an entire print run.

And I look on this from a sad and perplexed point of view, looking at *The Sandman* graphic novels, which . . .

You know, every quarter, I get my royalty statement for *The Sandman* graphic novels, and it stays the same, give or take, you know, a thousand here, a thousand there. But, basically, while the bottom has fallen out of the comics business and everyone else is down by a third, *The Sandman* graphic novels just sell and sell and sell.

And many of them now that sell through Barnes and Nobles and Borders, gradually, over the years they've noticed these things actually sell more than a Spider-Man graphic novel, or a Superman graphic novel, or a Batman graphic novel, and these become things that get automatically reordered, while Spider-Man, or Superman, or Batman graphic novels don't.

BB: *Right. So about how many are you selling?*

NG: Every quarter? Somewhere between 1,000 and 2,000 books. Of each title.

BB: *Of each title!?*

NG: [*Nods*] So that's somewhere between . . .

BB: *Ten or eleven thousand?*

NG: Well, twelve or fourteen [thousand], if you want to include *Black Orchid* and *Books of Magic*, as well. I've got fourteen books out there on backlist. They ship 1,000, 2,000, occasionally 2,500, if they can manage. They went out of print, so there was a little hiatus. Now they're back into print and doing two and a half [thousand per title], or whatever. That means that every year . . . That's about 80,000 books a year.

BB: *Do you think that's the future of the industry, packaging complete stories?*

NG: No, I don't know what's the future of the industry. I don't even know *if* there's a future for the industry. [However,] I think there will always be a future for the art work.

What *Sandman* demonstrated is that, if you told stories people wanted to read, they *will* read them. And they'll tell their friends about them, and get their friends to read them and . . .

On the one hand, it seems scary we've probably sold one million *Sandman* graphic novels; on the other hand, think of all the other people who've never read one, or don't even know they exist.

BB*: Or who have just discovered them because of the publicity on* Stardust, *and so on.*

NG: Yeah.

BB: *It must be interesting to have two almost completely different audiences; how surprising or different is that for you?*

NG: Not very. You know, I started in prose books, I middled in prose books, and, currently, I'm back in prose books. It's not that hard, it's not that different.

BB: *That's what I suspected; it might be a little different* *approach [depending on which medium you're working in], but you still just* write.

NG: Well, they're [the prose fans] a lot less likely to have a character tattooed on their arm, but that's because they don't have pictures of the characters.

BB: *Speaking of literature, would you agree with Harlan when he says that the Internet signals "the Twilight of the Word"?*

NG: No. But I think the Internet's a bother and a waste of time.

I was asked last night why I punched out Trent Reznor [of Nine Inch Nails]. And I had to explain that I didn't know why I had punched out Trent Reznor. And, for that matter, that I had never *met* Trent Reznor, although we have some mutual friends.

And I was told that I had *definitely* punched out Trent Reznor; it had been all over the Internet for ages now.

BB: *That's a new one to me.*

NG: It's a new one to me, too.

BB: *Just goes to show that it's an incredible source of information; sadly, it's mostly mis . . .*

NG: [*saying it simultaneously*] *Mis*information. Yeah.

BB: *I was just curious what your view would be, given that you and Harlan are somewhat close . . .*

NG: Oh, yeah; but Harlan still writes on a manual typewriter.

BB: *Yes. He's a glorious Luddite. It was very interesting to see the two of you working side by side at Mad Con. An interesting contrast.*

How about Neverwhere, *the film. Any news on that?*

NG: The film's at Miramax, their sort of science fiction-fantasy area.

BB: *And the Jim Henson studio is . . .*

NG: Producing it, yep.

BB: *You did the script, correct?*

NG: Yep.

BB: *And changes from the TV script, or from the book? Any major alterations?*

NG: Depends. I mean, by definition, the script for the film is an hour shorter than the script for the TV series.

BB: *Has it been cast yet?*

NG: No.

BB: *Do you have a "dream cast" in mind?*

NG: No. And those that I do, I don't tell anybody, because the last thing you want is—when you're approaching an actor's agent to say, "Would you like to be in such and such?"—for the actor's agent to say, "Yeah. By the way, we see that we're [part of] your 'dream' cast." You'd kind of want to go, "We'll offer you so much. We don't really want you." That's the typical way of doing it.

BB: *Yeah; I've been on that whole side as well. I know that there's been some media interest in* Stardust; *anything new to report?*

NG: We said no to Hallmark Movie of the Week, and we're currently in talks with people as diverse as Disney animation and Tom Cruise's [production company].

BB: *Ah. Yeah; I could see Tom as Tristan . . .*

NG: *No*; I didn't say that . . . although Nicole Kidman, I think she'd make a wonderful Star, if she'd do it.

BB: *Would you want to do the script, or would you trust another writer with it?*

NG: I don't know; I think probably do it myself. Only because, at least if I do it, it's me mucking it up. If someone else does it, you don't know *what* they do, and . . . They'll put in wacky bits and things.

BB: *I saw a recent quote from you stating that you had no connection with* The Sandman *movie, and that* Death: The High Cost of Living *was starting to look that way . . .*

NG: *Death* may happen yet; there's some light at the end of the tunnel, I think, but we'll have to see.

BB: *Would you still be directing that?*

NG: I would *desperately* hope so. I really don't want any-one else *but* myself. If anyone's going to muck it up, it should be me.

BB: *What about* Good Omens; *any media plans with that, since the millennium's coming up?*

NG: [*nods yes*]

BB: *Can you say anything at this point?*

NG: I can say that the Samuelsons—who did *Carrington* and the Oscar Wilde movie—have bought the rights; and I can say they have a director on board who may well be the perfect director for it. But I can say no more than that.

BB: *Script by . . . ?*

NG: By the director and by a writer he works with. Terry [Pratchett, his cowriter of *Good Omens*] and I, we went through that in 1990, and we don't want to go there again.

BB: *Can you provide any details on the TV pilot you're working on?*

NG: Nope.

BB: *I wanted to ask about the Dali film; what was acting like?*

NG: I'm still waiting for the phone call from Roger [Avary, the director]; every now and then I check in with him and ask, "Am I still doing this?" And he says, "Oh yeah."

BB: *So it hasn't . . .*

NG: Hasn't been shot yet. He's meant to be shooting sometime in the next few months. It's the sort of thing where he's not sure where he's going to shoot it, whether he's going to go all the way to Spain, or whether he can find somewhere in Mexico, or whether he's going to Toronto and try to fake it.

BB: *Is there a title on that?*

NG: The last script I saw had something like *Exquisite Corpse* on it, but I think he's going to be re-titling it till it comes out. I keep telling him he should call it *Hello Dali.*

BB: *Well, if he wants to sell it over here . . . And with that title, at least he'd get the musical crowd . . .*
What kind of role will you be playing? A large part, or supporting?

NG: I will be one of the surrealists.

BB: *And, of course, you won't know which one until you get there. [Neil nods] How appropriate.*

NG: Exactly.

BB: *I could see you playing [Jean] Cocteau, actually.*
How 'bout we move on to some more personal questions? What frightens you, both in real life and in horror or general literature?

NG: I don't know. Mainly the usual kind of things, you know. Uhm, that I'll be sitting in a railway carriage and suddenly be convinced that your eyes are just going to liquefy and roll down your face. Whatever. Things like that are particularly scary for me.

BB: *You* do *seem to have something for eyes. The Corinthian, etc., yeah.*

NG: [*nodding*] I get scared occasionally that I'll have to write the same thing over and over. I would hate it if *Stardust* were a big enough success that people would expect the next book to be a sweet fairy tale, or whatever.

BB: *You do seem to like shifting around a bit.*

NG: As long as I'm allowed to keep moving, I'm happy.

BB: *You've given up a number of things in recent years; for instance, you don't drink [alcohol] anymore . . .*

NG: Not so you'd notice; I just got very out of practice. I drank with enthusiasm all the way through my

twenties, but then, somewhere in my thirties, it stopped working in the same way. If I drank, instead of becoming smart, bouncy, relaxed, and the life and soul of every party, I would go straight to sleep. And it didn't take an awful lot of alcohol.

You know, I'd drink it down, and I'd fall asleep. And, after a little while, I stopped drinking. Because I would rather stay awake, and keep talking, than have a drink and go straight off to sleep. So I tend to think of drink giving me up than the other way round.

BB: *You've also given up . . .*

NG: Smoking.

BB: *And even coffee, it sounds like. So. What vices do you have? Writing?*

NG: Oh, writing, definitely. Uh, staying up too late, watching Jerry Springer at two o'clock in the morning on the satellite feed.

BB: *That must be an interesting cultural experience for you.*

NG: I actually miss the heyday of all of those daytime talk shows. What I used to like was, five years ago when I'd be writing at two o'clock in the morning, and I'd flip from the Richard Bey Show to Montel Williams to Jerry Springer to . . . various other people whose names have been swallowed by the mists of time. Whose names will be minor trivia questions.

BB: *So what do you do for entertainment, then, since that's behind you?*

NG: Well, I have small children. And I have large children. Between the two of them, one is rarely short of entertainment.

I like to get time to write. I like to get time to read.

BB: *So you're still able to enjoy it? Reading?*

NG: It's very hard for me to read fiction for enjoyment. The analogy I use when I explain it to people is that it's like being a stage magician going to see a magic show; you would not see the same show that the audience is seeing. They may be worrying about whether the woman is going to actually get cut in half, and you're admiring the smoothness with which he did the turn.

Having said that, there are still a few writers who can make me . . . who can pop me firmly back in the audience, and I don't get that at all with nonfiction. I love nonfiction.

BB: *Who are some of the authors you can still enjoy?*

NG: Jonathan Carroll. Stephen King; Steve can *always* pop me back in the audience. Gene Wolfe. And lots of dead guys.

BB: *Who were your favorites as a child?*

NG: Well, between the ages of seven and nine, it was probably C. S. Lewis. Then, from nine to fourteen, it was probably [Michael] Moorcock.

BB: *I suspected that, particularly after reading "One Life, Furnished in Early Moorcock."*

What's the typical day like for you when you're not on the road? In other words, I've always wondered how you and other writers with wives, and families, and real lives—such as you, Harlan, Peter David— manage to have a full family life and a career. So how do you balance the two?

NG: I have a little gazebo at the bottom of the garden which doesn't have a telephone in it. And the trick is simply getting out of the house and into the gazebo. If I don't get out of the house, the phone rings, and [suddenly everything becomes crazy]. If I do get out of the house, my assistant [aka, the Fabulous Lorraine] tells everybody who phones that she's sorry, I'm off writing.

BB: *Well, I'd imagine that one bonus about your success is the fact that you can do some traveling; and get away with your family and such.*

NG: Except that I didn't have that all through *Sandman*. *Sandman* was like one long drive. And even more recently, it's . . . Last year was traveling madness. This year, I've agreed to go to Finland and to Norway.

BB: *Back-to-back trips, right? For science fiction conventions?*

NG: Right. I'm not sure why, but I'm very popular in Finland and Norway.

BB: *Do you have any major media appearances slated for the near future? Perhaps* The Today Show, *or* Late Night [with David Letterman]?

NG: I tend to say "No" when I'm asked.

BB: *Why's that?*

NG: Because it's not about the personality; it's about the books. And I don't want to get out there, I don't want to be a celebrity. I don't like celebrity. I don't trust celebrity, and I don't want to be a celebrity.

You know, obviously, a certain amount of fame is simply the price for simply being read, and there seems to be no accepted way out of that if you are competent at what you do. Otherwise, you end up being a [Thomas] Pynchon or a [J. D.] Salinger, with people hounding you and invading your privacy all the time—*because* you are private.

So, I don't see that there's any easy answer to that, but I also feel you don't need to throw your petrol into the flames by turning up on [TV shows] and telling funny anecdotes. I don't mind talking to readers; but readers are different.

BB: *That's something I've noticed: you seem to genuinely enjoy your signings, which are really readings followed by question and answer periods, and then signing.*

NG: Exactly.

BB: *Can you think of anything else you'd like to add?*

NG: Nope.

Interview

Running Down a Dream:
Neil Gaiman on Stalking the Wild Tale

Even the most jaded observer of the comics and larger literary scene has to acknowledge that Neil Gaiman is an exceptionally accomplished writer. Since he entered the American market in the latter half of the eighties with his seminal series, *Sandman*, Gaiman's work has garnered accolades from fellow authors as diverse as Norman Mailer, Stephen King, and Harlan Ellison, and effectively captured the imaginations of an audience that literally embraces nearly every conceivable type of reader. Moreover, he's proven to be quite successful in other mediums, capable of extending his particular brand of narrative magic to encompass not only short stories and novels, but also television, radio, and film. And, as if that weren't enough, he's won just about every conceivable major and minor award and honor for his writing.

One fact that's often escaped notice, however, is just how prolific a creator he has proven to be. Despite the fact that he's only taken on one regular monthly assignment in his career, he's produced an amazing amount of comics. And the same holds true for his wider literary output, as just a glimpse at the flurry of recent releases—from the paperback versions of his phenomenally successful short story collection, *Smoke and Mirrors*, and his *New York Times* best-selling road trip novel, *American Gods*, to the wonderfully rich and quirky hardcover collection of his essays, short stories, and poetry, *Adventures in the Dream Trade*—bearing his name proves.

So the question remains, how does he do it? Moreover, why, after all of this time and prosperity, is he still working at his craft each and every day? Why is this phenomenally accomplished author still . . . Running Down a Dream?

Bill Baker: *When did you first become enamored with storytelling? Was there a particular moment that you remember it happening, or was it more of a gradual process?*

Neil Gamain: No. I think it was hardwired.

I remember, as a kid, I would daydream about being a writer at the kind of age when kids are *really* meant to daydream about being astronauts, or train drivers, or firemen. I *never* had any of those day-dreams. My daydreams were always, "Wouldn't it be wonderful to be a writer?" Only it never occurred to me I could do it by writing, because I was a kid, I guess.

But that is what I always wanted to be. Those were my daydreams.

I wish there was one cool, blinding moment that I could [point to and] say, "Before this, I didn't know that stories were what I wanted, and after it . . ." I think it goes as far back as I can remember, which is a very long way.

BB: *What about storytelling really appeals to you? Is it the whole act of creation, the fact that, in a sense, you're transforming reality?*

NG: No, I think a lot of it . . .

In many ways, the biggest thing, and the coolest thing, is creating something where there wasn't anything before. The magic of storytelling, you don't get to do it that often in your life, even as a successful writer, even as a fairly prolific writer. But, every now and then, you can give people stories that will change the way they see things. And that, of course, isn't why you do it. But that part is kind of cool, kind of strange.

The thing that I love is the way that *Dream of a Thousand Cats* [*Sandman* #18] didn't exist before I wrote it. And it was barely in my *head* before I wrote it. I knew I had to do a bunch of *Sandman* short stories, because I'd decided to do some short stories to get some ideas out of my head before I started the next big, long story line. And I was driving to the railway station, which happened to be at Gatwick Airport. It's about a half hour drive through narrow country roads. And I saw a large cat sitting on the side of the road, very big, and very, very black, just looking like a little patch of night. And I thought, "You know, if the Sandman was a cat, *that's* what the character would look like." And I thought, "*There's* a story! I think I'll tell that one." The following four or five days later, I sat down and wrote it in a weekend. Which might sound incredibly odd, because normally it would take me something in the region, at that point, of about two to three weeks and, later on, four to five weeks to write a *Sandman* story.

Like I say, it's that moment of creation, the moment where there wasn't something where you began and now, suddenly, there's something cool that is. I suppose [stories are] always like a kid. You know, they grow up, and go out in the world, and do their own thing. And that's what I love about stories, because they do that, too, sometimes.

BB: *When did you actually start writing things down?*

NG: God, I remember when I was around three getting my mum and dictating a poem to her—it wasn't very good, no surprise—and making her write it down. Telling her, "You write this down!" And she did. And then, as a kid, English [class] was what I loved. English essays, stories. And it was fun. I'd get to write. I'd get to sit there in English pretending I was Robert E. Howard, or whoever I was reading that week. I mean, I'm a nine-year-old writing Michael Moorcock stories, or whatever.

And then, when I was about thirteen, I started doing comics. I'd just write and draw these fairly terrible comics which, by the time I was about fourteen, they were sort of [looking like the work of] somebody who wanted his stuff to look like Barry Smith, but couldn't be bothered to learn all the drawing stuff underneath. So I'd do all the sort of odd Barry Smith–shaped noses, or Barry Windsor-Smith, as he wasn't yet known at that point. And then . . .

It's very odd right now. A few nights ago, I just ran out of things to read to my daughter, who is seven. Suddenly I remembered that I'd written a kid's book, a kid's novel [called *My Great Aunt Ermintrude*], when I was about twenty-one, and went and did a quick hunt in the attic, and found it. It was the very first thing, full-length thing, I'd finished. I'd sent it off to a publisher at the time, and got it just as smartly back, and said [to myself], even at the time I'd gone, "This is one of those 'first novel' things. Everybody should write a first novel and put it away." So I did.

But I pulled it out to read to Maddy because I figure after twenty years you can't be embarrassed by things you did wrong, and things you didn't know how to do, and I couldn't even really remember the plot. I've been reading it to her, a few chapters a night, and what has been fascinating is that I expected to be mortified and embarrassed all the way through. [But,] actually, what I wound up doing is being incredibly, pleasantly surprised every time a twenty-one-year-old me did *anything* good. Which was actually quite often.

Like I said, I had no idea at all about structure. I also had *no* idea about doing a second draft. I sat there and wrote the book in handwriting, and then typed it out and taught myself to type at the same time. And actually, because I finished writing the book before I finished this "Teach Yourself Typing" manual I'd bought myself, I'm still, to this day, about a six-finger typist because I only got up to about lesson six and then it was time to start typing my book. I often wish I'd finished the manual.

BB: *I was just thinking about some of your past interviews, and in one of them you were talking about the fact that it's sometimes hard to tell, afterwards, what were the easy parts and what were the rough patches when you were working on them.*

NG: [*laughter*] When you're working, you have *no* idea. And when you're working, and you're actually doing it, you're out there in the swamp, trying to jump from a little tussock of earth and dry ground to another little tussock three or four feet away, knowing between you and that tussock there is nothing but quicksand. And it's a very nervous, strange, awkward jumping *thing* at which the possibility and the probability of failure, and eternal distraction, is lurking behind everything.

From a distance, for other people and, in fact, in memory, it *doesn't* look like you're stumbling through a swamp. It looks like you are striding confidently through what is obviously solid ground. And, of course, you're not.

For me, the strangest of all of those is my book *Coraline*, which comes out this summer [September 2002]. It's a short novel, 30,000 words, which is exactly half the length of an adult novel. It's a book that, literally, took me ten years to write. I wrote a big chunk of it in 1990 and '91, the first 8,000 words, and then wasn't sure what happened. And then picked it up again sometime in about '97, and did the next 2,200 words between then and April–May 2000, sometimes doing 50 words a night.

At one point I was meant to have seriously begun *American Gods*, and I'd arranged for a train journey to San Diego. I *love* long train journeys, because nobody can even get a hold of you. Your mobile phone doesn't work, so you're off and you're working and there's nothing else you can do. And I got on the train and I discovered the *American Gods* stuff that I was meant to take with me wasn't with me. So I had three days of traveling, and quietly wrote *Coraline* through that. And even once I'd finished it, in 2000, my English editor felt there was a chapter missing. She said, "What happened to *this* character?" And I said, "Ah. You know, you're right!" I knew, and I never put it in there. So I settled down in October of last year and wrote the other chapter in a couple of days.

And the only reason I'm talking about the incredibly long, convoluted, peculiar way this thing was written is, it's *seamless.* You wouldn't look at it and go, "This was written in these tiny fits and starts and peculiar lumps over a period of, quite literally, ten years. Maybe eleven." You sit there at the beginning, and read it all the way through to the end, and it seems so much of a piece that the building process behind it is invisible. And frankly, when I was doing the copy editing last week—the galley proofs came in and I gave them a read through—and it was invisible to me. It was just all, very obviously, all one thing, one story.

Does that clarify that?

BB: *Quite a bit. And it leads to the next question, which is that you seem to have a very different writing*

Trinidad High School
· Library

process than is typically taught, especially in America.
We're often told as students that you have *to outline*
everything beforehand, and get it all nailed down
beforehand, and then *you write it.*

NG: I did that *once*. I did it with *Black Orchid*, and didn't
really enjoy it terribly. I mean I liked it insofar as it
felt like all I had to do was write the scenes one after
another. I wouldn't get up in the morning not knowing what the next scene was. On the other hand, there
was precious little fun in it, and there wasn't any
moment that I surprised myself in *Black Orchid*. I
may have surprised myself towards the end. Book
Three, I think, may have felt a little strange. I may
have done stuff that wasn't actually in the outline, I'd
have to go back and find it to see. Basically it was all
planned out, it was all outlined.

My favorite outline moment was when I wrote a
Babylon 5 episode for Joe Straczynski, called "Day of
the Dead," a couple years ago. Joe had been after me
for five years to write him an episode, and I *finally*
had time. And I said, "OK, I can do it!" I said, "I've
got an idea," and I told him my idea. And he said,
"Hm, I like that. Let me run it by the producers." He
rang me back the next day and he said, "I ran it by
the producers. They like it." And I said, "OK, great.
Shall I write you an outline now?" And there was a
pause. Joe said, "Do you *like* writing outlines?" And I
said, "*No*." And he said, "Neither do I." And I said,

Trinidad High School
Library

"In which case, I have one question." And he said, "Forty-three pages," without missing a beat.

Outlines, I think, are fun when they're *useful*. Like with this Marvel thing (*Marvel 1602*) that I'm currently doing, or just about to start. I'm putting together, before I actually start writing, I should have a little map of, more or less, what occurs in each of the six issues. Only because I don't want to suddenly get to issue five and realize that I now have another four issues worth of stuff to do. Which is what I tended to do in *Sandman*. Which is something that you have that liberty to do in a monthly comic like *Sandman*. I'd start something and I'd go, "Oh, I think this is going to be like five issues long." And then, all of a sudden, you look up sixteen months later and you've done *The Kindly Ones*.

BB: *Well, why don't we talk about your writing process? It really is kind of an act of exploration for you, isn't it?*

NG: Mostly, yes. It drives editors nuts.

A lot of the time it can be an accumulation. You are thinking about things, planning things. If you know you're writing a story about something, everything that you run into that seems to be concerned with that pops in your head into a sort of box with that kind of shape.

I'm right now doing a *Sandman: Endless* short story collection (*Sandman: Endless Nights*), which is kind of fun. The *first* thing for me, on that, was knowing who my artists were, because in each case knowing the artist then shaped what the story was going to be. The first story I had to do was a Death story. I knew I had *Moebius*. Moebius seemed perfect for Death, and I was running through various ideas in my head. And then I wound up spending about a day and a half in Venice on my way to Trieste earlier this year, immediately after September the 11th, when the planes started flying again. And I was having a conversation with somebody in Trieste, and they were talking about "empty islands," some of these islands in the lagoon that are empty. And the day before I walked into a book shop, and noticed a little Moebius sketchbook of drawings of Venice.

And *that* sort of combined in my head with some stuff I'd read about five years ago. I found myself reading *The Memoirs of Casanova*, and actually wound up reading them twice. I read the first round because it was translated and written by a guy called Arthur Machen, a writer I like. And then I realized that he was working from an expurgated text, and the complete text was only around now. Most of it was expurgated for reasons of religion, not of sex, but I read them again. These huge, thick books. Actually, thinking back on that, I think I had an appalling case of flu, so I was stuck in bed for a couple of weeks, sniffling and drinking hot lemon. So I had a very, very good sense of Venice in the 1750s from that, and thought it might be very interesting [to use].

And then, when I was walking through Venice, I wound up having a conversation on a bridge with a man who had a little boom box playing and, next to it, dancing on air, a little paper Mickey Mouse and Minnie Mouse. He tried to sell me them, telling me that they were magnetically charged paper dolls, at five dollars each, and they would dance on air. And I told him it looked actually like they were dancing on an invisible monofilament, and being jiggled up and down by a motor in his shopping bag placed next to the boom box, and he suggested that I go away.

And I thought, "There's a wonderful metaphor." You know, things dancing on invisible strings. And I thought, "Now, *that's* a *Sandman* metaphor if ever I had one." And, at that point, it was merely a matter of writing the story. I knew, when I sat down, that it was a story with all of those things in it. I knew that it was *for* Moebius, and that it would have a sort of strange correlation of walking and moving backwards and forwards between the 1750s and now. The thing is, writers use phrases after that, like, "And after that, it just wrote itself," which tries to make light of the fact that you then, in my case, spend about fourteen-fifteen days trying to craft that material into a story, and getting the beats, and understanding *why* it's a comic. And writing *very* nervously for Moebius, who is, after all, a genius.

And, as soon as you're finished, it looks like you were striding confidently through that swamp. It doesn't look like you were jumping from tussock to tussock. [*general laughter*] And I wound up writing a story I was *really* proud of; of a man, in the here and now, who may or may not be a military assassin—we're never quite sure—who winds up on this deserted island where he went once as a small kid and encountered Death, and this strange palace on the island where they just have this one day in 1759, over and over again.

BB: *Do you still typically work on the computer when writing?*

NG: It depends. For me, writing is a process of outwitting the process of *not* writing. And computers these days, more and more, are designed to be entertainment boxes. And the more a computer is designed to be an entertainment box, the easier it is for me to write on other things. Or, failing that, to write it out.

I have a little office now, which I finally gave in and got a few years ago, which is not [connected to] the phone. So when I take my computer out there I can't plug it into anything, which is great. Here in the house, all the computers are plugged in to the Internet, and that's plugged in to some satellite upload and download system, and any attempt to write in the house is doomed. Because the first time I want to check the spelling of an obscure word and go dig through dictionary.com, I'm then off following an interesting trail of whatever, and no work is getting done.

Like I say, for me the process is one of outwitting the process of *not* writing. So, when I moved from a typewriter to a computer, that was great, because paper wasn't getting dirty, and there was a magnificent freedom that anything I wrote was imaginary until I pressed the "Save" key. And I liked that. These days, I'm much more likely to start in a notebook. I'm much more likely to have a fountain pen, and a little notebook, and to start writing there. Because now I'm at the point where nothing's real until I've actually started typing it in.

BB: *Has that changed your work? I ask, because I'm thinking of* Stardust, *and how that book turned out.*

NG: *Stardust* was the first time I'd every actually gone, "Right. I'm writing this in long hand." I think, *particularly* with *Stardust*, it changed the way that I thought sentences through. I wanted to write archaically. But then, I wound up doing the first draft of *American Gods* pretty much in longhand, in big notebooks, and I don't think you can tell.

When you're writing comics, for me, as well, you *need* a pen. Because I keep doodling out panel breakdowns, doodling out page breakdowns, looking at ways to tell the story. [Working out questions like,] "How many panels do I want per page? What kind of thing am I doing here? Am I trying something interesting? Is it gonna work?"

I'm trying something right now with this Milo Manara story, which I'm writing for the [new] *Sandman* book, which, when I'm done writing it, I may well do a final draft on the script—which is one of the nice things about computers—where I get rid of it altogether. Because I thought it would be really interesting to have a character in the story who keeps talking to the reader. Instead of doing it all in captions over [the art], I thought, "Wouldn't it be interesting to have somebody who's talking to us?" As if we were an invisible camera, sort of continually breaking the fourth wall, as it were.

So I'm trying that right now, and I *think* it works. But I may well wind up sending it into Karen [Berger, his editor at Vertigo] and having her say, "This really isn't going to work." And me going, "No, I didn't think so," and going back in and just making it all captions, rather than speech balloons addressed to the reader. On the other hand, it may be fun. At least it's different.

BB: *Do you still create* ashcans *of everything, as far as comics are concerned?*

NG: Yep. Well, I *say* ashcans. You get four sheets of paper, fold them over, and you now have a little [version] of what the comic is going to be. You sit there and draw it all out. Actually, this *Sandman* book, I've been doing them in a big old notebook. Crossing it over, you know, four [comic pages] to a page.

But it always tells me, for example, some of the basics of comics, which is always [concerned with things like,] "When are you making somebody turn a page? When does their eye flick up? When are they turning a page? What are they turning a page *to*? Why?"

BB: *When you're moving from one format to another, from a short story to a screenplay, from an introductory essay to a novel or a comic, how much of a shift do you have to make mentally? Does that take some effort, or does it all seem to be just storytelling, and you just fit it to the format?*

NG: There's a quote from Roger Zelazny in the beginning of the *Books of Magic* collection, where he says,

"Editors think they're buying the story, but actually they're buying the way the story is told," and each of those things gives you a different vocabulary in the way the story's told. Oddly enough, some of the ones that get *closest* to each other for me are, for example, radio plays and comics. One of which is all visual, and the other has no visual track at all, and yet [both] have a very, very similar writing process. Short stories and novels are, on the whole, a very similar process for me, although novels are still ones I feel I have so much to learn on.

It's very strange right now. I was sent this list from *Locus* magazine, a science fiction magazine—they have an online [version], I think it's www.locusmag.com—and they've been keeping track of all the "Year's Best" lists. And *American Gods* has made it on to more "Year's Best" lists than any other book this year. Which may just be because it was a thin year. I looked at that and I thought, "That's just wonderful. Just wait till I have it figured out, this whole novel idea. Wait till I get one right!" [*general laughter*]

American Gods, I liked at least some of it. I felt that I'm getting there, I'm starting to understand what I'm doing. And it was actually fun in *American Gods* because I actually stole a bunch of things from *Sandman*. There's all these *things* I made up while I was writing *Sandman*, including moving into short stories whenever I needed to comment on the main text, and inform it, while not actually keeping that story going, and doing these strange little historical short stories. [So] I thought, "Well, I'll do some of that in this novel," and did, which was great fun. But, again, I don't actually feel yet that I've figured out the craft of writing the novel, and I have quite a way to go.

Short stories are fun because you can see the end of them when you begin. Normally, for me, a short story is actually in the tone of voice. If you have an idea, and you have a voice for that idea, whether it's a narrative voice or a character's voice, you pretty much have a short story.

BB: *It's almost literally transcribing what they're telling you, then?*

NG: Yeah. Well, that implies there are mysterious voices out there sort of talking to you and you're not doing it. Of course you're doing it.

But, very often, if you have a character's voice, or you have a narrator's voice, whatever medium you're in you can navigate your way through. It's the equivalent of the walking stick for that mysterious and mythical swamp we were talking about at the beginning. Those short stories that I've written the first page of, or paragraph of, and never got back to, tend to be because the voice is wrong, or tend to sometimes be because the voice isn't right, or the tone isn't right for the story. Sometimes it's fixable.

In the case of children's books, there's a book called *The Wolves in the Walls*, which I should hope comes out in the next eighteen months. I finished it about two years ago, and it sits waiting for Dave McKean to get the time to do sixty drawings for it. *The Wolves in the Walls* is a book where I had the idea for the story and tried writing the story once, and it didn't work. And I wrote the whole thing all the way through. And it was short enough, and it was a kid's book, [that] I thought, "You know, what I think I'll do is try again in about six month's time." And six months after that I sat down and wrote three or four paragraphs and thought, "Naw, that's not it yet." And six months after that, I thought, "I think I have an idea now. I think I know the tone of voice," and sat down, and just wrote it either that afternoon, or over two days, all the way through.

And I have no idea if it took me seven hours to write. I think it probably took me three or four *years* to write. But a lot of that three or four years was just figuring out, somewhere on the inside, what the story sounded like, what the narrative tone of voice was. It's very, very dry. It's very flat. You know, *The Day I Swapped My Dad for Two Goldfish* is told by the kid who swapped his dad for two goldfish, pretty much from his point of view. *The Wolves in the Walls* [uses this] just wonderfully dry sort of narrative voice, which is, "I'm un-surprised by *anything*. Even the fact that there's wolves living in the walls of this girl's house."

BB: *It works wonderfully live. I was lucky enough to be at one of your readings when you pulled that piece out.*

NG: Oh, good. It's one of those things that's very, very funny live. And it's very funny *because* the narrator never makes any jokes. [*general laughter*] The whole story is completely deadpan.

And, as I say, it took me as long to write it, more or less, as it does to read it. But there's at least one complete, and several incomplete, attempts to write it before that, where I knew what the story was, but I just didn't hit the tone. And, sometimes, that's the best way of doing something. Sometimes you have to be willing to put a story aside, to say, "It doesn't work. But there's something there that does work. I'll come back and I'll try it again," and *not* to look at the early drafts when it's time to start again, not to look at your notes. Just to assume that it's been quietly composting down in the back of your head.

BB: *I know that you usually have two or three things you work on simultaneously, and had been wondering how* *you moved between them. So you don't necessarily look at what's come before, but just dive right back in where you left off, and continue writing at that point, when you return to a piece?*

NG: Yeah. [*laughter*] I say that; that's not necessarily true.

If I'm on the computer, normally I'll look something over. Maybe not from the beginning. Maybe from a page or so from before, and I'll fiddle with it, as my way of getting back into it.

In the old days, I'd find it easy to have two very, very different things sitting there. Two big, full-length things. Now, what I'm tending to do . . .

Well, for example, yesterday I was out in my little cabin working with a Milo Manara story I'm writing on one screen, and the introduction I'm doing to the next edition of *The Hitchhiker's Guide to the Galaxy*—they're bringing it out as sort of a memorial to Douglas [Adams] edition—and I'm Guest of Honor this year at the World Horror Convention in Chicago, with Gene Wolfe as a fellow Guest [of Honor], and I was asked to write an appreciation of Gene. And what was fun is I had all these things up as different windows on the computer, different screens in the word processing program. And I'd do the Manara thing until I got stuck or grumpy with it, and I'd flip to one of the others and write another paragraph about Douglas or another paragraph about Gene. And it meant that instead of going off grumpily, doing

those things writers can do instead of writing, like having another cup of tea, or suddenly deciding that the wallpaper in the bathroom needs stripping, or whatever it is you can imagine, I'd just do a little of something that's not quite the same thing, and that would keep me going. And it was something else that needed to be done.

There are people out there, like Stephen King or Terry Pratchett, the guys who . . . They're not even simply professionals: they're the antithesis of what Douglas Adams was. Douglas was a man who would spend *years* not writing books, and who took a certain amount of miserable satisfaction of only being able to write at that point in the day when he'd had as many cups of tea as you could possibly have, and as many baths as you could possibly have, in a day. And only *then* would he begin to write. Whenever his life was not boring, he wouldn't write.

There are people out there who are very, very good at just really getting down and doing their pages every day. I'm, constitutionally and temperamentally, one of those who would love to be a Douglas Adams. And, if it wasn't for starving, [I might be]. I manage always to persuade myself to be one of those people who say, "Well, you have to do your thousand words a day. If you do a thousand words a day, then in a hundred days time, you'll have a first draft of a novel." "Well, OK." Or a hundred and eighty days for a first draft, whatever. I can do *that* kind of thing and keep going. I only really get in trouble when I have too many projects on the go, and I'm over-committed, and not assigning my time right.

But I've watched writers and artists over the years who really *do* need somebody breathing down their neck. There's an artist, who I shall not name, who I worked with first about twelve years ago on *Sandman*, who quit because he didn't like the way that he was being pestered to make deadlines, and felt, as an artist, that he should deliver stuff in his own time. He went off to another comic company and found an editor who was very simpatico with him, and he had a graphic novel to do, a hundred-page graphic novel. And, as the years went by, he worked on this graphic novel. Whenever I'd see him he'd show me whatever the few pages he'd done that year were, and tell me very proudly how these guys didn't pester him for pages. About seven years later, the editor was fired, and the graphic novel *still* wasn't finished. And the guy realized that A) It was not finished, and B) He was *never* going to finish it now, because nobody wanted it. And ten years had passed, and he hadn't actually done anything or had anything published. And it's easy for that to happen, too.

Starvation is very good for stopping that from happening. But if starvation is not the problem, then it can be all too easy for a writer or an artist to *not* work. And also, I sometimes think, for many of the artists and writers I've run into, the *worst* thing is the quest for perfection.

There was a colorist who I wanted to work on *Sandman*. We got him the black and whites for *Sandman* #1, and he was meant to produce some color guides. [But] they weren't perfect, so he never turned them in. He finally showed them to me, about the point that *Sandman* 3 came out, and it was being colored by somebody else. The first guy was better, but he never got to work on it because he had been off on some strange quest for perfection that didn't actually involve produced stuff.

So there always comes a point where you go, "Is this perfect, or . . ." And it *never* will be, so you may as well move on. Get it as good as you can, and then keep going. Maybe the next thing, maybe you'll get it right *next* time.

BB: *How do you tell when your stuff is at that point? Is it almost like a "click" in your head when you look at the work, or is there some other way to tell?*

NG: Normally, for me, what actually happens is I get obsessed by the next thing. I can always tell when I'm near to finishing something, because I'm not worrying about it anymore. I'm worried about the next thing down the line. [*laughter*] But, there's also a level on which, when you make art, you don't particularly spend your time worrying about whether you made art. I mean, you shouldn't. It's much wiser to be willing to move on.

With *Sandman*, when a story was twenty-four pages long, and it seemed to be done, I'd send it in. Because by that point I was already worrying about what's in the next one. Writing a novel, again, I just sort of [notice,] "Now I'm starting to get worried about what the next novel's going to be." That's a very good place to be. Just sort of thinking about it.

And also knowing that the place where most of the magic gets made is on the page. I suppose this goes back to that very first thing we were talking about right at the beginning, those things where you surprise yourself, where you're creating something from nothing. If I had to point to the one thing about being a writer that's the coolest, it's that magical moment *between*. It's the point where you turn a corner; you have a character walking down a corner, and you suddenly realize that, oh, darn, you've got some other characters walking down that street as well, and if he turns that corner right now, he'll run into them. So you suddenly remember, "Oh, god, I *need* to keep him talking on this corner!" and somebody walks up to him and, all of a sudden, you have this wonderful scene. And you have no idea of where it came from. It wasn't planned. It wasn't anything. It wasn't in your head a moment before, and now you're typing it, and you get to be the first audience.

I *love* that moment.

BB: *You mentioned that there are some things in* American Gods *that you weren't entirely happy with earlier. Is this something that's typical for you, a sense that there's always something, some aspect of the work that could have been better?*

NG: Oh, yeah. Except *occasionally.* I mean, *Coraline* I don't think I can improve. But *Coraline* is one of a very, very small number of things that I've done where I have *no* idea of how I did it. I don't think I could ever do it again. I'm not sure I can ever do anything quite like it again. It was barely crafted, and it came out of whatever the place [is] that the dreams come from. Writing it in the way that I wrote it is *obviously* a recipe for disaster.

If I were told, "OK, start a novel now that you will finish when you are in 2010, when you're fifty-one, and keep the same narrative voice," I'd be going, "It's not going to happen!" Yet this is a novel I began when I was thirty and finished when I was forty-one. And I have *no* idea how I did it. So that one I look at as this weird kind of *thing* that I'm happy with it, because I wouldn't *know* how to change it. [*laughter*] I don't quite know what to do with it.

But *American Gods* is something that I *built*, and I built it day by day for almost two years. I look at it and I go, "Well, it would be nice, in a perfect world, I think it could have been about a third again as long." It would have been even longer, even more rambling, even more intricate, had more strange diversions. We would have gone to more places and met more things. And there's an alternate universe in which I carried on writing it for three years, instead of two. It may not have been a better book in that universe; it's certainly a bigger one. And I sometimes regret that, just because I just had so much fun writing it, and meeting all these people.

[Actually,] that's kind of an unthinking comment to say, I think. "I had *such* fun writing it!" In actual fact, I probably had fun writing it one day in three. [*general laughter*] But, looking back, again, it's that "striding solidly from tussock to tussock" thing. You're going, "Oh, yes, it was wonderful. Easy process of writing." And, of course, it wasn't.

When I was working on it and people would say, "Well, how's it going?" I would say, "Well, it's a lot like wrestling a grizzly bear. Some days the grizzly bear's on top. Some days I'm on top." And I was just secure in the knowledge that if I kept wrestling for eighteen months, at the end of that time I would have a book. Whether it would be a good book or not, I really didn't know. It seems like most people like it, which is very nice. It got wonderful reviews, and made the *New York Times* best-seller list in hardback, and looks set to do it again in paperback, and all of these things are nice. But there was an awful lot of gorilla wrestling in there.

BB: *What are some of the things that you haven't had a chance to do yet that you're interested in doing someday?*

NG: Plays. I haven't done any live theater.

I woke up a couple of days ago with a *structure* in my head. Sometimes, a lot of the time, *structure* will give me the shape of the story. And, sometimes, I even wind up abandoning the structure. *Sandman* #6, *24 Hours*—the horrible one set in the diner—came from a desire at that point, [of me] going, "You know, I'm in a twenty-four-page comic; wouldn't it be cool to do a story called *24 Hours* in which I do one hour per page?" And then, of course, I wound up abandoning that structure slightly, because I needed six pages to set up the first hour, and many of the later hours were done in half pages. But that was the idea. I just liked the idea of doing these beats, hour by hour, through a story. And the story it generated was this nightmarish, monstrous story that probably wouldn't have existed if I hadn't of thought of the structure.

[Anyway,] I woke up the other day with a structure in my head for this wonderful stage play for five characters. Actually, there are six characters, but one of them isn't there. And I thought, "Oh, well that would be so cool to write! When am I going to have time to write it?" I figure, well, maybe 2004, probably 2005. And suddenly some of the fun went out of it.

I'd *love* to do stage, I'd love to do live theater. There is a real, particular magic that happens in live theater that doesn't happen in any other context.

Beyond that, I'm not sure. I *wish* there was a tradition of radio theater, of audio plays and stuff, in America. Which there really isn't. It got interrupted in the late 1930s, and what you tend to have since is faintly nostalgic. One of the nice things about England is the BBC maintained the tradition of radio plays, which is how you get people like Douglas Adams. *Hitchhiker's Guide* was a radio show, that's what it began as. Radio is such a wonderful, vital force, and such a [good] way to do things cheaply. It's so much quicker and cheaper.

When I did my first radio play for the BBC, there was a point where we had to do a scene once, and then we knew that we were going to cut back into it, and we wanted it to be much more distant. So we did it once, and then we did it again with everybody standing three or four paces away from the microphone. And I thought, "You know, if we did that in a movie, we would have just lost half a day for setups, re-lighting the scene, and moving all the cameras. It would have went away just like that!" [*general laughter*] And it took us twenty seconds; we moved everybody three steps back from the mike. I'd love to do more audio plays.

I was very happy, for a couple of years, when the Sci Fi Channel Web site was doing these "Seeing Ear Theater" things. I did one starring Brian Dennehy and one starring Bebe Neuwirth. So I got two Tony Award–winning actors; in fact, Bebe got two Tonys, so I now had a grand total of three Tony Awards in my things, which was fun. And, unfortunately, "Snow, Glass, Apples" with Bebe was the last one that they ever did, because somebody noticed that these things weren't actually generating any money. They were merely only generating good will.

BB: *What about film, are you excited about the possibilities there?*

NG: No. [*general laughter*] But I'm writing film.

I'm currently working on a movie for Robert Zemeckis, and working on *Death: The High Cost of Living*, and there's at least five, maybe more, projects of mine—stories, novels, comics projects—that are out there currently being transformed into film or not. But having knocked around in Hollywood for too long, [I know that] everything costs too much money. Everything involves too much waiting, indecision.

The joy for me of writing a book is, if I write a book, that book will be written. When I finish *American Gods*, I do a second draft on it, and then the book comes out.

Currently I'm working on an animated project for DreamWorks, for example. They came to me and said, "We have this classic story we'd like retold as an animated film. Would you do us an outline for it?" So I did. Then I did them another outline. Then I did them another outline. Then I did them another outline. Then I said I wasn't doing any more outlines, and they said, "Can we give you more money to do more outlines?" And I said, "I guess." [*general laughter*] So they threw a year's wages of a high school teacher at me, and I'm doing more outlines on this project, which I think will be fun.

But what is frustrating for me is where I would actually wind up creating it, where I make it live and where I make it work, would be writing the script. That's the bit for me that is fun. And they want everything tied down beforehand, which I guess is their right, because they know that, when it goes beyond an outline, they have to pay me a large chunk of money to write a script, and stuff like that. And then they have to get the concept drawings done. And, from start to finish, even if we get a green light this week when I hand in the outline . . . Which, actually, now that I come to think of it, was the other thing I had up on my screen yesterday while I was writing. [*laughter*] I thought there were two big things, not just the Manara stuff. The Manara, this outline, and Douglas Adams and Gene Wolfe introductions.

It'll be five years until this thing is made. And I will probably be fired from the project at least once, and lots of other people will come in and write lots of extra dialogue and what have you. And this may just wind up creating art, and it may not. It may be a good movie, and it may not. But the things that will make it a good movie are not necessarily anything to do with me sitting writing my outline, or me writing my script. Which may sound slightly apathetic, but I think it's essentially more practical. One of the things I love about comics, I love about radio plays, I love about short stories and novels: if it works, it's my fault. If it doesn't, it's my fault. And with films, if it works, god knows whose fault it is.

BB: *Right. It could just be the editor, for all we know.*

NG: There are many films in which it *is* the editors. And there are many films in which the editors are not to blame.

I remember seeing the editor's cut of the first episode of *Neverwhere*, which made a lot of sense, and was really exciting, and worked, and was just sort of really good. And then I saw the director's cut of it, which he liked, and I didn't, and was the one broadcast. And I thought, "Isn't that interesting? The material was the same, more or less, although different takes were sometimes used. But the way that you build it together was completely different." So, yes, it could well be the editors.

BB: *What do you look for in a project that's not something you generated, say something like the upcoming* Marvel 1602 project, *or the animated film you were just discussing? What does it take for something like that to interest you enough to become involved with it?*

NG: Pardon me, but the Marvel project *is* something that I generated. The Marvel project was very much for me a reaction to a bunch of stuff that was going on, particularly September the 11th, [and me] thinking, "Well, it'd be nice to do something that's not about this stuff."

What tends to happen is there's *something* in there that seems like it's gonna be fun. Occasionally, when I'm stuck in the middle of some complicated project, looking around, blinking, and I'm going, "Well, why did I get involved in this?" the answer's always the same. Which is, "It seemed like a good idea at the time." Actually, thinking about the DreamWorks project, the DreamWorks project had the same rationale that several other things that I've been involved with over the years had, which is, "At least if I screw this up, at least I'll screw it up with love." Which is, more or less, what got me into *Princess Mononoke,* and was the reason I decided all those years ago to give *Black Orchid* an origin. I thought, "Well, somebody's going to do this. It may as well be me, because I'll do it as best as I can." [*laughter*]

And, in the case of the Zemeckis project, it's something I said "No" to for several years. It's [based upon] a book that Bob loves. And [then] I reread it, and realized why he loved it, and I realized it's all about one scene toward the end. And he flew out to Minneapolis. We had this meeting at the airport, in this little conference room, and I said, "It's all about this one scene, isn't it?" And he said, "Yeah." And I said, "Oh, OK. So I can more or less throw away the rest of the book, can't I?" He said, "Yeah." And I said, "Because the only way I can do it is like this: blah, blah, blah, blah." And he said, "That's what I want!" And I said, "Oh. OK, good." And, thrilled by my own cleverness, I signed on. And then I went on my own and thought, "What have I got myself into?" But I'm enjoying it.

BB: *What do you think is really lacking in much of comics today?*

NG: I don't know.

The thing that I've always wished with comics is just that there were more. More comics for more people, more different kinds of comics.

I *never* disliked superhero comics, but I always figured that superhero comics were a very small genre. What was fun [about] doing *Sandman* was, more or less, creating a genre, going, "OK, we can do fantasy comics. Look, let's do one of these things." You know, if I were doing it all over again, or if I were starting again, or if I were going to spend another five years just working exclusively in comics, I think I'd try and create more genres. Just go off and do stuff that nobody has done, necessarily. I'd love to see less reliance on superheroes comics as the commercial mainstay of comics. Which, like it or not, at the end of the day they are.

I think the only thing that I wish a lot of the time is that people who are good writers would write less.

I remember once getting into an argument with a writer, who I shall not name, who's another Vertigo writer, while I was working on *Sandman*. I was saying that it would take me roughly a month to write a *Sandman* script. This writer was incredulous, and explained that he or she took a *maximum* of twenty-four hours to write a script for his or her comic. And explained to me very carefully that, financially, you *needed* to write however many comics it was, in however much time it was, and they worked it out mathematically. So it was a very specific thing, "OK, you can afford to spend [X amount of time on a script]." And this person was explaining to me that I was mad.

At the time, I was getting $2,000 a script, something like that. I was making $2,000 a script, and there were a few thousand dollars coming in on royalties, but I didn't think it was particularly *bad* money. It wasn't wonderful money, but I was surviving on it, it was fine. And it was explained to me that I was nuts, and financially the only way that it could possibly work was to do twenty-four hours [of work, total,] spread over three days, however long to write the script.

And I stopped the other day and thought about it. And I thought, "Well, everything I ever did doing *Sandman* is still in print." The books are now in their eighth, ninth, tenth printing. They sell, year in and year out, somewhere between forty and eighty thousand copies a year. *Every* year.

BB: *And that's every individual volume, correct?*

NG: Yeah. They just keep selling, and selling, and selling.

And I did the sums, and I thought, "You know, in actual fact, *Sandman*, which people didn't laugh at or sneer at, but nobody was aware of or thought of as a commercial success when I did it, if you take the trade paperback sales since, and spread them back over [the series' run]—you said, 'OK, this is what we actually sold over seventy-five issues'—each issue of *Sandman* by now would have sold one and a half *million* copies." You know, we would have been doing 1.5 million over seventy-five issues! [*general laughter*] And I thought, "Which is better than any other comic would have ever done. Even at the height of the Image thing, that was for a couple of comics here or there. But we did it over seventy-five." And I thought, "Actually, I did the right thing." Just quietly nestling down and taking as long as it took to get it right, and not going, "Well, I have to write X amount of things, otherwise I starve!" And there are writers out there who are capable of *terrific* work, and who are capable of *beyond* terrific work, and I go, "Well, I wish you were doing one, or maybe two projects. Look, you're writing five monthlies!"

I should probably clarify here that I'm very specifically *not* referring to Alan Moore. Who, I think, whatever he's doing at ABC is very much about writing fast comics, and just creating this wonderful, strange, self-sustaining world of *Promethea*, and *Tom Strong*, and what have you.

But that, in terms of writing, is one of those things that I tend to wish. Which is that people would write a little less, and write a little better. The people who are capable of it.

BB: *I know you've been asked this question a number of times, but, considering the venue this piece will appear in, I think it's appropriate to ask it yet again: What do you think that those people who want to become good writers need to keep in mind?*

NG: There's a bunch of different things that somebody who wants to be a writer should keep in mind, and there are different kinds of advice you give to different people. To most people, the best advice you can give somebody who says, "I want to be a writer," is *write*. And *finish* things. Because that's very often going to separate 95 percent, or even 99 percent, of the men from boys. Do you want to be a writer? Great. Write. You want to be a writer, and you have hundreds of unfinished beginnings of things in drawers? Great. Finish things. A lot of the time, that's all it'll take.

Beyond that, you're into sort of much more the second-stage advice. Read everything you can, and read the kind of stuff you *don't* like. I'm very grateful that for my early twenties I was a book reviewer. I had to read *everything*. I was not the kind of book reviewer who only got to read one kind of thing. I was reading everything, and it was *great*. Because I got to read all sorts of books I would *never* have gone out and paid money for. Wonderful.

The other thing that I would advise is, if you're capable of writing, and you're technically good, and you can finish things, but you don't necessarily have anything to say, is, "Good, go and *live*." Go do things. Go experience the world. Sign up on a tramp steamer, if they still have tramp steamers. I loved being a journalist in my early twenties. It was great, because you got to mix with every level of the world. It gave you a very interesting perspective.

Get out there. Go places you wouldn't otherwise go. Do things you wouldn't otherwise do. And get your heart broken. Make a mess of things. Triumph over adversity. Great. Now come back. Well, at least you have something to write about.

And it's not going to be *those* things. You're never going to wind up taking the stuff you've experienced and plunking it straight on the page. At least I hope you won't. But, by this point, the batteries should be charged. There is material.

Now, that's the kind of advice you give somebody who's got everything else *but* that. Most people, you never get to the point of giving that piece of advice. Because most people who want to be writers, they want to be writers but they want elves to come in the middle of the night and write for them. Or they want elves to come in the middle of the night and finish things for them. Or they're sure if you just start a novel, and put it in a drawer, it'll keep writing itself in the darkness.

BB: *And they all seem to end up becoming producers in Hollywood, don't they?*

NG: Many of them do. [*assumes a pitch-perfect Hollywood drawl*] "Hey! OK, Neil Gaiman. We love you, we love your stuff. Now, we have this kind of idea, OK? And we just want you to, like, do that thing you do to it? OK. So, the idea is—wait for it—it's like *Faust*, but we want, like, computers in there."

[*as himself*] "And the idea is?"

[*in the Hollywood voice*] "No, that's the idea! Kinda like *Faust*, but computers in there. I don't know. Upload, download, you're the writer!"

Right.

BB: *Do you want to talk about artists for a bit?*

NG: Absolutely. What would you like to know about artists?

BB: *What do you think makes a good artist? The reason I ask is because I know you have such a strong and* *varied knowledge of, and interest in, artists whose styles range from Mike Diana to Moebius and back.*

NG: Yeah, absolutely.

What makes an artist, for me, is some kind of personal vision, something I can tap into. The only artists that I don't particularly think about working with tend to be those guys who are the superhero artists who are *so* generic that nobody notices when they're not working anymore, if you know what I mean. The ones who you don't even quite have time to register that they're this year's, or this month's hot artist because they're not in comics anymore and, anyway, their style is the same as the last guy's. Those kind of people *tend* to leave me fairly cold, because I can't see what I can bring to it.

What I like is an artist with a personal vision, because at that point, even though the artist isn't necessarily involved with plotting, you are collaborating. You are collaborating with an artistic style. When I was talking about putting together a story for Moebius, a lot of what I put into the story had to do with what I wanted to see Moebius draw.

Right now I'm doing a story for Milo Manara, and I began by listening in my head to things I want to see Manara draw. And some of them are things he draws anyway. Beautiful women. There had to be beautiful women in it. There had to be beautiful women in various states of undress in this story because Manara loves drawing that. *But* there's all sorts of other things that I want to do, as well. And some of them, I'm going, "Well, the work of Manara's I enjoyed the most was probably *Indian Summer*," which he collaborated with Hugo Pratt on. That beautiful historical stuff. And I'd love that kind of texture in there. And, furthermore, I remember that Fellini thing he did [*Journey to Tuluum*], and it would be nice to get that kind of *intensity* of vision in there. So you're sort of already going, "Well, this is stuff that he's done that I'm interested in. What have I *never* seen Manara do?" And you go, "Well, there's stuff in here that I could probably get away with in terms of long-haired people hitting each other with swords," which I would never have given, say, to the late John Buscema if I'd had him drawing, because it would have been all cliché. But I'm going, "Manara never draws this! If I do this, he's actually gonna draw . . ." and at that point, you're thinking differently. You're thinking both for and against type.

For me, the most important question for any artist when I was starting a *Sandman* thing is . . . I'd always want to talk to any artist who was doing a long story line, and I'd say, "What do you like drawing? What do you want to draw that nobody's ever written for you?" And sometimes that would be enough.

BB: *What do you hope that your readers get from your work? Obviously, you hope that there's a few moments of entertainment there, but is there anything else outside of that?*

NG: I'd like, I suppose, to color their days. To change things a little. To make a very, very small amount of magic or difference.

I always hope that people who read *Neverwhere*, for example, would go to England, and travel on the tube, and look up at the names on the tube, and go, "My god, these were in that book!" and wonder. With *American Gods*, a lot of it was just a feeling of, "This is the America I've been living in for ten years. Here are my eyes. This is what it looks like from in here." [*laughter*] Once you've seen it through these eyes . . . [For] some people it makes good audio, or whatever, and some people may think me this strange English person, and people may read the book and go, "Oh, I always wanted to put that into words." With *Sandman* it's the strangeness of actually having created something that may in some ways outlive me, and outlast me. It's much more interesting than some guy making up stories somewhere.

BB: *Any last words?*

NG: No, no. I don't have any last words. Or, at least, I hope not yet. [*general laughter*]

Interview

The Last Guardian Angel Visitation:
Neil Gaiman on the Comic Book Legal Defense Fund (CBLDF) and the Last Guardian Angel Tour

Between readings of his now-classic short stories and poetry (such as "Chivalry" and "Nicholas Was"), and performances of new material (including *The Wolves in the Walls*; his second children's book, "A Prayer for the Blueberry Girl," which was written to celebrate the birth of musician Tori Amos's first daughter; and "Coming to America," one of the short stories he uses as a narrative device in his epic road trip novel, *American Gods*), Neil told the audience about the facts behind current efforts to suppress free speech in comics, the Constitution-shredding case of Mike Diana, and his own personal experiences with censorship.

Still, a central question remained unaddressed: Why does he care so much? So I decided to ask Gaiman why he's become such a vocal champion of the First Amendment, and why the author of the critically acclaimed *Sandman* series would care what a court in Florida had to say about a small 'zine and its creator. His answers reveal a side of Gaiman that has often been overlooked: specifically, his passionate determination that comics—regardless of their content, genre, or apparent artistic merit—be given the same rights and range of expression as all the other arts.

Bill Baker: *Why did you start the Guardian Angel Tours, and why are you calling a halt to them?*

Neil Gaiman: Well, it started, more or less, accidentally. It was about 1993, and I got a call from the owners of the Beguiling, a comic store in Toronto. And they said, "Why don't you come up here? We'll rent a theater, and sell tickets for the [Comic Book] Legal Defense Fund, and you can do a reading for the Defense Fund." And I said, "Are you *sure* this is a good idea?" And they said, "Yeah! Joe Matt'll buy a ticket if you do."

    So I said OK. And I went and did the reading, and it was a huge success. We sold [out] a 500-seat theater, and I discovered that I'm good at it. I think Susan Alston, from the Legal Defense Fund, had come up to help to organize it, so she then put one on in Northhampton [Massachusetts], at the Northhampton Theater, and that went brilliant. And, really, we've just been doing them ever since. And it turned into this two-weeks-a-year tour, where I do a few locations, take [over] a little theater, and do readings. And I enjoyed it no end.

The problem was just finding two weeks [free time where I could do it]. Finally, at the beginning of this year, I said to Chris Oar, the director of the fund, "I can't do it. I can't keep doing it. I'd like to go on holiday with my children before they grow up and leave home. Finding two weeks a year to go on tour is becoming impossible."

"*And*," I said, "I'd also love to see more people moving in and filling the kind of ecological niche that would be created if I were to vacate. If I stop doing this, maybe other people would start getting out on the road, doing their own thing for the fund."

So, that was why we decided to do the last one, and make it a huge one, make it a big one. Which it is. It's four stops: Chicago, New York, Portland, and L.A.

BB: *Does this signal the end of your involvement in, and your efforts on behalf of, the fund?*

NG: No, absolutely not! It just signals . . .

I just feel like seven years of going out on the road is enough. It felt like the time. And I've always been very fond of the idea of finishing in a big way when you're at the top, rather than limping on until everybody's sick of you. It was the way that we did

Sandman. And it seemed like a very good thing to do now.

BB: *So we'll be seeing more things like the recent e-Bay auctions [during which Neil's famous black leather jacket was sold for four figures]?*

NG: Yeah. I'll do more e-Bay stuff. I'll probably get much more directly involved with the fund itself. But, in terms of actually gettin' out there and educating people for $20 a ticket, I probably won't. This [will be] the last of the tours. It may not necessarily be the last time I ever actually get out in front of people and entertain them for the Legal Defense Fund, and tell them stories, or read them poems. Or it may turn out to be, if I do this again, it may turn out to be . . . I may actually go on the road as a support act for, ya know, Led Zeppelin reforming. I could get out there and read stories as a support act for that one.

I'm not necessarily saying this is even the last time I get out and tell stories in public. But it feels like it's time to be done. And, again, I'd like to see more people gettin' out and doing stuff like this, themselves.

BB: *What sparked your interest in the Fund in the first place? I mean, come on,* Sandman *is not Boiled Angel [Mike Diana's 'zine that a Florida prosecutor, judge, and jury found so offensive that they not only fined*

Diana heavily, but mandated police searches of his residence without any warrants to enforce a ruling that he could not produce art of any kind in the future . . . despite the fact that both violate Diana's Constitutional rights].

NG: *Sandman* is not *Boiled Angel*. Having said that, and this occurred in about 1995 or '96, well after I became involved with the Defense Fund, in Gainesville, Florida, the chief of police went into a store [nearby] and said [to the owner], "OK, you're selling this thing, *Death: The High Cost of Living*, and it has this seven-page thing in the back, called 'Death Talks About Life,' . . . and they talk about . . . how not to get AIDS. How not to get pregnant. How not to die." She said, "I don't like this. I don't want you selling this. And, if you keep on selling this, I will put you out of business." And the store owner very sensibly got in touch with the Legal Defense Fund, and the Legal Defense Fund attorney fired off a letter. And the police department laid off [the store].

Freedom of speech, as far as I'm concerned, is an absolute. Americans seem to treat freedom of speech in the same way the English treat the Health Service. The English have the National Health Service. If you're a poor person in England, and have heart problems, you will get treated. It will not financially ruin you for the rest of your life. Or you will not have to choose between getting the heart [problem] treated, and eating. If you are severely injured in England, you go to the emergency room. It's something you take for granted. And people [there] grumble about it. They're not really sure if it's very good or not, but they do. People actually take it for granted.

In America, you have guaranteed freedom of speech for everybody. This is one of those cool things, like health care, that people take for granted when they've got it. And I think that's why, as an Englishman, coming out here [I can appreciate that right]. Saying that "*Sandman's* not *Boiled Angel*," as far as I'm concerned, diminishes the obscene behavior of the Florida court in regard to *Boiled Angel*.

Imagine that, instead of being a comics artist and writer, Mike Diana had been a novelist. And if a novelist had been [found] guilty of obscenity, and been convicted to three years suspended sentence, a $1000 fine, psychiatric treatment at his own expense—which is something Soviet Russia was really into, enforced psychiatric treatment of dissident artists—a course in journalistic ethics at his own expense, [and] he's not allowed within ten feet of anyone under eighteen—he lost his job at a convenience store—and not allowed to draw anything that might be considered obscene, with the local police authority instructed to make twenty-four-hour spot checks (without need of a constitutionally required warrant) on his place of abode, to make sure he wasn't writing, *if* that was a novelist doing that, Amnesty International would have taken that one up. He would have been on the [front page] of *Time* magazine. It would have been a cause celebre.

Instead, a few comics people know about Mike Diana. A few civil rights and First Amendment people know about the Mike Diana case.

And I remember being completely shocked when, some years ago, at a convention in Charlotte [North Carolina], where I was there as a guest of the Legal Defense Fund, and I was doing one of these readings, and I had asked for Mike Diana to come in and introduce me [to the audience], and the convention organizer wouldn't let Mike Diana's name be written down anywhere. They wouldn't let him be mentioned over the loudspeakers. It was as if he deserved it, he brought it on himself, for drawing pictures that other people didn't like.

I'm sorry, freedom of speech is an absolute. The rule is, if you don't like the pictures, you don't look at them.

Let me limit that; freedom of speech to *adults* is an absolute. Freedom of speech to kids isn't. But, then again, *Boiled Angel* was *not* being sold to kids. The person it was sold to, who was the person who made the complaint, was a police officer pretending to be a fanzine fan. And I suspect that, if he was anything like the police officers I know, was reasonably unshockable.

But, there ya go. Sorry about the rant.

BB: *No need to apologize. This is information that, as you know, most people aren't aware of, but really* need *to know about.*

Well, given the current climate, and an increasing tendency towards censorship in this country, what are your thoughts on labeling of comics? Do you have any suggestions or solutions in this area?

NG: I wish people would label intelligently.

Frank Miller and Alan Moore are hard-line anti-labeling people because, as they point out, very successfully, that it doesn't seem to do much good. A retailer in Texas was convicted six weeks ago of selling a comic labeled for over eighteen, [which was racked] in the over eighteen section of the shop, to an undercover cop who was over eighteen. As they [Miller and Moore] said, "Sure helps a lot!"

I think that intelligent labeling is probably a good thing. I only think that because there are some very stupid people out there, and there are some very stupid television reporters and such out there.

If you hand a child a box of DC comics, everything they published that month, they will go through it and pull out the ones that look appealing. And that *won't* be *Transmetropolitan*, and it *won't* be *The Dreaming*. It'll be *The Batman Adventures*, stuff that *looks* like it's for kids. And, frankly, if you give your typical *Wizard* [magazine] reader that same box, they will probably ignore *The Dreaming*, *Lucifer*, and so on and so forth, as well. Again, because they don't *look* like people in colorful spandex punching each other. On the other hand, you give that box to an eighteen-year-old, they'll probably go through and that'll be the stuff they'll pull out, because they're done on the spandex.

So, I think there's a level on which stuff self-selects anyway. Very few comics "light up" in people's hands. And, as many people point out, bookstores . . .

You don't go into a bookstore and see age limits, and stuff, on the back of books, and labeling. On the other hand, things are labeled in bookstores by the way that they look, and by the place where they're positioned.

BB: *And also by the publishers' suggestions [concerning genre, age group, etc.].*

NG: Well, yeah, but I'm not even thinking of "Recommended for three to nine year olds" [suggestions]. 'Cause you have to *look* very closely for those, and they're certainly not for a lot of things.

But I am saying that you can pretty much tell, wandering around a bookstore, what kind of stuff you'll probably like, and what kind of stuff you won't. And, unfortunately, there is a long tradition in the world of the media of getting a bunch of comics . . .

I remember one thing done with *Elektra: Assassin*, the wonderful Frank Miller/Bill Sienkiewicz strip. They held up *Elektra: Assassin* to the camera, and then pulled back to see a display of *Teenage Mutant Ninja Turtles*, and *Archies*, and stuff, it was a sort of a kid's section, and they said, "*This* is what your kids are reading! I bet you thought comics were this, but *this* is what your children are reading!"

BB: *Any last thoughts on what an average reader can do to help? I mean, a Neil Gaiman can go on tour, but what can your average reader—as an individual—actually* do?

NG: Well, an average reader can become a CBLDF member. That's the basic, most simple thing. Twenty-five dollars a year, it gets you a card. The card gets you into a bunch of CBLDF events. For my reading tour, for example, a CBLDF membership card will get you into the sort of pre-show mingle, meet-and-greet cocktail party thing, which otherwise you have to buy $60 VIP tickets to get into. So, they'll do all kinds of cool, magical things.

Other than that, you can do simple fund-raising. Somebody once pointed out that if every comic shop in America had a jar in the front, you know, the kind of jar people drop pennies, and spare change, and stuff like that into for the fund, and got it off, it would triple or quadruple the fund's revenue.

And the other thing somebody can do in the short run is come on out to one of the readings, in the Chicago, New York, Portland, or L.A. area.

For more information or to donate to the Comic Book Legal Defense Fund, visit it online at http://www.cbldf.org or call (212) 679-7151.

Selected Works

Over the course of the past two-plus decades, Neil Gaiman has written an incredible number of comics, original graphic novels, illustrated books, short stories, novellas, novelettes, and novels as well as journalistic pieces and other works of nonfiction. More recently, he has further expanded his reach by writing screenplays and scripts intended for various media. Therefore, the list that follows is by no means comprehensive. However, it does provide a wide-ranging sampling of Gaiman's rich catalogue of work.

Novels, Collections, Illustrated Books, and Graphic Novels Intended for All Ages

Coraline. Illustrated by Dave McKean. New York, NY: HarperCollins, 2002.

The Day I Swapped My Dad for Two Goldfish. Illustrated by Dave McKean. New York, NY: HarperCollins, 1997.

MirrorMask. Illustrated by Dave McKean. New York, NY: HarperCollins, 2005.

M Is for Magic. New York, NY: HarperCollins, 2007.

The Wolves in the Walls. Illustrated by Dave McKean. New York, NY: HarperCollins, 2003.

Prose Novels and Collections Intended for Teens and Older Readers

American Gods. New York, NY: William Morrow, 2001.

Anansi Boys. New York, NY: William Morrow, 2005.

Fragile Things. New York, NY: William Morrow, 2006.

Neverwhere. New York, NY: Avon Books, 1997.

Smoke and Mirrors: Short Fictions and Illusions. New York, NY: Avon Books, 1998.

Stardust, the Novel. New York, NY: Avon Books, 1999.

The Sandman Graphic Novel Series and Related Titles Intended for Teens and Older Readers

The Absolute Sandman. Illustrated by various artists. New York, NY: Vertigo, 2006.

Death: The High Cost of Living. Illustrated by Chris Bachalo. New York, NY: Vertigo/DC Comics, 1994.

Death: The Time of Your Life. Illustrated by Chris Bachalo and Mark Buckingham. New York, NY: Vertigo/DC Comics, 1997.

Dustcovers: The Collected Sandman Covers 1989–1997. Illustrated by Dave McKean. New York, NY: Vertigo/DC Comics, 1997.

The Sandman: Book of Dreams. New York, NY: HarperPrism, 1996.

The Sandman: The Dream Hunters. Illustrated by Yoshitaka Amano. New York, NY: Vertigo/DC Comics, 1999.

The Sandman: Endless Nights. Illustrated by various artists. New York, NY: Vertigo/DC Comics, 2003.

The Sandman Vol. 1: Preludes & Nocturnes. Illustrated by various artists. New York, NY: Vertigo/DC Comics, 1991.

The Sandman Vol. 2: The Doll's House. Illustrated by various artists. New York, NY: Vertigo/DC Comics, 1990.

The Sandman Vol. 3: Dream Country. Illustrated by various artists. New York, NY: Vertigo/DC Comics, 1991.

The Sandman Vol. 4: Season of Mists. Illustrated by various artists. New York, NY: Vertigo/DC Comics, 1992.

The Sandman Vol. 5: A Game of You. Illustrated by various artists. New York, NY: Vertigo/DC Comics, 1993.

The Sandman Vol. 6: Fables & Reflections. Illustrated by various artists. New York, NY: Vertigo/DC Comics, 1993.

The Sandman Vol. 7: Brief Lives. Illustrated by various artists. New York, NY: Vertigo/DC Comics, 1994.

The Sandman Vol. 8: World's End. Illustrated by various artists. New York, NY: Vertigo/DC Comics, 1994.

The Sandman Vol. 9: The Kindly Ones. Illustrated by various artists. New York, NY: Vertigo/DC Comics, 1996.

The Sandman Vol. 10: The Wake. Illustrated by various artists. New York, NY: Vertigo/DC Comics, 1997.

Graphic Novels Intended for Teens and Older Readers

Black Orchid. Illustrated by Dave McKean. New York, NY: Vertigo/DC Comics, 1991.

The Books of Magic. Illustrated by various artists. New York, NY: Vertigo/DC Comics, 1993.

Creatures of the Night. Illustrated by Michael Zulli. Milwaukie, OR: Dark Horse, 2004.

The Eternals. Illustrated by John Romita Jr. New York, NY: Marvel Comics, 2007.

The Facts in the Case of the Departure of Miss Finch. Illustrated by Michael Zulli. Milwaukie, OR: Dark Horse, 2007.

Harlequin Valentine. Illustrated by John Bolton. Milwaukie, OR: Dark Horse, 2001.

The Last Temptation. Illustrated by Dave McKean. Milwaukie, OR: Dark Horse, 2000.

Marvel 1602. Illustrated by Andy Kubert. New York, NY: Marvel Comics, 2004.

Mr. Punch: The Tragical Comedy or Comical Tragedy. Illustrated by Dave McKean. New York, NY: Vertigo/DC Comics, 1994.

Neil Gaiman's Midnight Days. Illustrated by various artists. New York, NY: Vertigo/DC Comics, 1999.

Neil Gaiman's Murder Mysteries. Illustrated by P. Craig Russell. Milwaukie, OR: Dark Horse, 2002.

Signal to Noise. Illustrated by Dave McKean. Milwaukie, OR: Dark Horse, 1992.

Stardust. Illustrated by Charles Vess. New York, NY: Vertigo/DC Comics, 1998.

Violent Cases. Illustrated by Dave McKean. Milwaukie, OR: Dark Horse, 1991.

Other Books of Interest by Neil Gaiman

The Alchemy of MirrorMask. Illustrated by Dave McKean. New York, NY: Harper Design, 2005.

MirrorMask: The Illustrated Film Script of the Motion Picture from the Jim Henson Company. Illustrated by Dave McKean. New York, NY: William Morrow, 2005.

Selected Awards

Over the course of his storied career, Neil Gaiman has been the recipient of numerous prizes and honors from a startling number of international associations, groups, and organizations spanning a dizzying array of fields. Therefore, the following list, which concentrates on U.S.-based awards, is by no means comprehensive.

American Library Association Award
2006

Best Book for Young Adults for *Anansi Boys*

August Derleth Award for Best Novel of the Year
2006
Anansi Boys

Bram Stoker Awards for Superior Achievement (in Horror)
2003
Best Illustrated Narrative for *Sandman: Endless Nights*

2002
Best Work for Younger Readers for *Coraline*

2001
Best Novel for *American Gods*

1999
Best Illustrated Narrative for *Sandman: The
    Dream Hunters*

Harvey Kurtzman Awards (for Achievement in Comic Books)

1993
Best Continuing/Limited Series for *Sandman*

1992
Best Writer for *Sandman*

1991
Best Writer for *Sandman*

Hugo Awards (also known as the Science Fiction Achievement Awards)

2004
Best Short Story for "A Study in Emerald"

2003
Best Novella for *Coraline*

2002
Best Novel for *American Gods*

International Horror Guild Award

1994
Best Collection for Angels and Visitations

Locus Readers' Poll Awards

2004
Best Novelette for "A Study in Emerald"
Best Short Story for "Closing Time"
Best Nonfiction/Art Book for *Sandman: Endless Nights*

2003
Best Short Story for "October in the Chair"
Best Young Adult Novel for *Coraline*

2002
Best Fantasy Novel for *American Gods*

Mythopoeic Awards (for Outstanding Work in the Fields of Myth, Fantasy, and the Scholarly Study of These Areas)

2006
Fantasy Award for Adult Literature for *Anansi Boys*

1999
Fantasy Award for Adult Literature for *Stardust*

Nebula Awards (for Best Science Fiction/Fantasy)
2003
Best Novella for *Coraline*

2002
Best Novel for *American Gods*

Will Eisner Comic Industry Awards (for Achievement in Comic Books)
2004
Best Anthology for *Sandman: Endless Nights*
Best Short Story for "Death" from *Sandman: Endless Nights*

2000
Best Comics-Related Book for *Sandman: The Dream Hunters*

1994
Best Writer for *Sandman*

1993
Best Continuing Series for *Sandman*
Best Graphic Album: New for *Signal to Noise*
Best Writer for *Miracleman* and *Sandman*

1992
Best Continuing Series for *Sandman*

Best Single Issue/Single Story for *Sandman* #22 to 28
 Season of Mists
Best Writer for *Books of Magic*, *Miracleman*, and
 Sandman

1991
Best Continuing Series for *Sandman*
Best Graphic Album-Reprint for *Sandman: A Doll's House*
Best Writer for *Sandman*

**World Fantasy Award (for Outstanding Achievement
in the Field of Fantasy)**
1991
Best Short Story for *Sandman* # 19 "A Midsummer's
 Night Dream"

Glossary

accolades Signs or expressions of praise.

adversity Hardship or suffering.

anecdotes Short biographical, interesting, funny accounts of incidents or events.

antithesis The complete or exact opposite of something or someone.

apathetic Having or showing little interest or emotion.

archaically Relating or belonging to an earlier time period.

cameo A small role, often limited to a single scene, by a well-known actor or character.

cliché Something that has become overused and has therefore lost its original power or effectiveness.

clout Influence.

convoluted Too involved or complex to understand easily.

dissident Expressing or showing disagreement with authority or the prevailing opinion.

enamored Having a strong interest or fascination with something; charmed or captivated by.

expurgated Having had harmful, unsuitable, or offensive parts or passages removed before publication.

flagship The finest, largest, or most important among a
group of chain stores or other similar, related things.

garnered Collected, earned, or accumulated.

harlequin A character in pantomime and comedy who
has a masked face; a clown.

harlequinade A play or performance in which a harlequin has a leading or prominent role.

hiatus A period of time during which something is interrupted or suspended.

Luddite One who is opposed to technological change.

mandate An official command or instruction from an
authority.

monofilament A single untwisted strand of fiber such
as nylon, often used for fishing line.

moratorium A waiting period or suspension of activity.

niche The role of an organism in a community.

petrol British word for gasoline.

pyramid scheme A usually illegal operation in which
participants pay to join and profit mostly from the
payments of subsequent participants.

seminal Influential.

simpatico To be on the same wavelength; sharing similar
temperaments or interests and therefore getting along
well together.

surrealist One who produces fantastic or dreamlike
imagery or effects in art, literature, film, or theater by
means of unnatural combinations and juxtapositions.

tramp steamer A ship that operates without a schedule but goes wherever required to deliver its cargo.

tube The London subway system.

tussock A small thick clump of grass or sedge (a wetland plant).

unscrupulous Without moral or ethical principles.

untenable Not able to be defended (as a position); not able to be occupied.

urbane Showing sophistication or refinement; polite and polished in manner.

For More Information

The Comic Book Legal Defense Fund

271 Madison Avenue, Suite 1400
New York, NY 10016
(212) 679-7151
Web site: http://www.cbldf.org

Dark Horse Comics

10956 SE Main Street
Milwaukie, OR 97222
(503) 652-8815
Web site: http://www.darkhorse.com

DC Comics

1700 Broadway
New York, NY 10019
(212) 636-5400
Web site: http://www.dccomics.com

HarperCollins Publishers
10 East 53rd Street
New York, NY 10022
(212) 207-7000
Web site: http://www.harpercollins.com

Marvel Publishing, Inc.
417 5th Avenue
New York, NY 10016
(212) 576-4000
Web site: http://www.marvel.com

Vertigo
1700 Broadway
New York, NY 10019
(212) 636-5400
Web site: http://www.dccomics.com/vertigo

Web Sites

Due to the changing nature of Internet links, Rosen
Publishing has developed an online list of Web sites related
to the subject of this book. This site is updated regularly.
Please use this link to access the list:

http://www.rosenlinks.com/twgn/nega

For Further Reading

Bender, Hy. *The Sandman Companion: A Dreamer's Guide to the Award-Winning Comics Series.* New York, NY: Vertigo/DC Comics, 2000.

Kwitney, Alisa. *The Sandman: King of Dreams.* San Francisco, CA: Chronicle Books, 2003.

McCabe, Joseph. *Hanging Out with the Dream King: Interviews with Neil Gaiman and His Collaborators.* Seattle, WA: Fantagraphics, 2005.

Olson, Steven P. *Neil Gaiman* (The Library of Graphic Novelists). New York, NY: Rosen Publishing, 2004.

Rauch, Stephen. *Neil Gaiman's the Sandman and Joseph Campbell: In Search of Modern Myth.* Rockville, MD: WildSide Press, 2003.

Sanders, Joe, ed. *The Sandman Papers: An Exploration of the Sandman Mythology.* Seattle, WA: Fantagraphics, 2006.

Schweitzer, Darrell, ed. *The Neil Gaiman Reader.* Rockville, MD: WildSide Press, 2006.

Index

Acknowledgments

Bill Baker would like to take a moment to thank . . .
First and foremost, Neil Gaiman, for his energy, kindness,
vocal support of my efforts, and especially that most
precious of all commodities, his time.

Neil's assistant, the Fabulous Lorraine, who justifies the
modifier before her moniker each and every day.

Neil's agent, Merrilee Heifetz, and her assistant, Claire Reilly-
Shapiro, for all of their help in making this particular book
not just possible, but also infinitely easier.

All the good folks at Rosen Books, especially Kristin Eck,
Iris Rosoff, and Elizabeth Gavril, who have provided valuable
guidance and insightful commentary while seeing this
book to press; Nicholas Rook and his team for the fine design
work; and Roger Rosen, who brought me into the fold.

Finally, you, the reader, for picking up this volume and making it all real once again, if only for a fleeting moment.

You've all helped make this an entirely pleasurable and truly rewarding experience. I am indebted to each and every one of you, in ways both large and small.

Thank you.

About the Interviewer

Over the course of the past decade, veteran comics journalist Bill Baker has contributed interviews and feature stories, reviews, and news reportage to various magazines, including *Cinefantastique/CFQ*, *Comic Book Marketplace*, *International Studio*, *Sketch,* and *Tripwire*. During that same period, Bill also served as an interviewer and reporter for a number of Web sites, including www.ComicBookResources.com and www.WizardWorld.com. These days, when he's not working on his latest interview book, Bill serves as the host of "Baker's Dozen" for www.WorldFamousComics.com.

Bill currently lives and works in the wilds of the Upper Peninsula of Michigan, for some unknown and quite likely complicated reason. You can learn more about Bill's activities, past and present, by visiting his blog at http://specfric.blogspot.com and his professional Web site at www.BloodintheGutters.com.

About the Interviewee

Neil Gaiman is an incredibly popular and multiple award-winning author of comics, children's books, original graphic novels, nonfiction books and prose novels, radio plays, short stories, and television and movie scripts, as well as poetry and sundry other entertainments. After getting his start as a journalist and reviewer in his native England, Gaiman soon turned his attention toward comic books, and it was the DC Comics series *Sandman* that eventually cemented his reputation as one of the most original creators to have ever worked in that field. Since then, he's gone on to pen a string of *New York Times* best-selling books, including *American Gods* and *Anansi Boys*. Currently, Gaiman resides in the Upper Midwest of the United States, surrounded by family, friends, a library of mystifying proportions, and a veritable herd of cats.

Series Design and Layout

Les Kanturek

TRINIDAD HIGH SCHOOL
LIBRARY